A Dorset Childhood

Growing up in the land of the Tolpuddle Martyrs at the time of the Cold War

ANDREW NORMAN

ryelands

Dedication

To my Dearly Beloved Wife
Alison Rachel Norman:
The Love of My Life
The Light of My Life
My Precious Lamb

First published in Great Britain in 2023

Copyright © Andrew Norman
Cover design: George Kalchev

All rights reserved. No part of this publication may be reproduced, stored in a retrieval system, or transmitted in any form or by any means without the prior permission of the copyright holder.

British Library Cataloguing-in-Publication Data
A CIP record for this title is available from the British Library

ISBN 978 1 906551 53 7

Ryelands
Halsgrove House,
Ryelands Business Park,
Bagley Road, Wellington, Somerset TA21 9PZ
Tel: 01823 653777 Fax: 01823 216796
email: sales@halsgrove.com

Part of the Halsgrove group of companies
Information on all Halsgrove titles is available at:
www.halsgrove.com

Printed and bound in India by Parksons Graphics Ltd

Acknowledgments

Dorothy Bower; Nicola Brooke; Anne Burman; Norman Carey; Tony and Barbara Coombes; Nigel Costley; Gabriel Drágffy; Katalin Drágffy Simon Gooch; Tony Gould; Roger Guttridge; Stuart Hannabuss; Christopher Hazelwood; Robert Heathcote; Jeff Hogarth; Elisabeth Jordan; Peter Medhurst; Nicola McConnell; Bob Penrose; Barbara Pierce; Simon Sheppard; Graham Stevenson; John Tory; Michael Walker; Tom de Wit.

Country Standard; Dorset History Centre, Dorchester; Library & Knowledge Service, Poole Hospital, University Hospitals, Dorset; Peoples' History Museum, Manchester; Somerset & Dorset Family History Society; TUC Library Collection, Special Collections, London Metropolitan University.

Maps of Bryanston and Blandford Forum reproduced by courtesy of Ordnance Survey and Trustees of the National Library of Scotland.

Sources:

Bristol Evening News.
Country Standard.
Daily Worker.
Deutscher, Isaac, *Stalin: A Political Biography,* Penguin Books, 1966.
Dorset County Chronicle.
Dorset Echo.
Dorset Standard.
Dunman, Jack, 'Food and Farming', The Communist Party, London, 1963.
Izvestia.
Jordan, Arthur, *Away for the Day: The Railway Excursion in Britain, 1830 to the Present Day*, Silver Link Publishing, Kettering, Northamptonshire, 1991.
Jordan, Arthur, *The Stratford-upon-Avon and Midland Junction Railway: The Shakespeare Route*, Oxford Railway Publishing Company, Headington, Oxford, 1982.
Land and Labour.
Landworker.
Loveless, George, *The Victims of Whiggery: A Statement of the Persecutions experienced by the Dorchester Labourers*, Effingham Wilson, Strand, London, 1837.
O'Connor, Kristine Mason, *Joan Maynard: Passionate Socialist*, Politico's Publishing, London, 2003.
Petrovics, Istvan, 'Transformations in Contemporary Europe since 1945. East-Central Europe', in Szentirmai László (szerk.): ERASMUS előadások/The ERASMUS LECTURES (válogatás/selection) 1998-2003. I. Szeged. 113-120.
Poole Herald.
Pravda.
Salisbury Journal.
Stevenson, A., and Waite, M., *Concise Oxford English Dictionary*, (Oxford and New York, Oxford University Press, 2011).
Sutcliffe, Jennifer, *Face: Shape and Angle*, Manchester University Press, 2016.
The Book of the Martyrs of Tolpuddle: 1834-1934, The Trades Union Congress General Council, London, 1934.
Western Gazette.
Western Morning News.
World News & Views.

By the same author

By Swords Divided: Corfe Castle in the Civil War. Halsgrove, 2003.
Thomas Hardy: Christmas Carollings. Halsgrove, 2005.
Enid Blyton and her Enchantment with Dorset. Halsgrove, 2005.
Tyneham: A Tribute. Halsgrove, 2007.
Agatha Christie: The Finished Portrait. Tempus, 2007.
The Story of George Loveless and the Tolpuddle Martyrs. Halsgrove, 2008.
Father of the Blind: A Portrait of Sir Arthur Pearson. The History Press, 2009.
Agatha Christie: The Pitkin Guide. Pitkin Publishing, 2009.
Arthur Conan Doyle: The Man behind Sherlock Holmes. The History Press, 2009.
HMS Hood: Pride of the Royal Navy. The History Press, 2009.
Purbeck Personalities. Halsgrove, 2009.
Bournemouth's Founders and Famous Visitors. The History Press, 2010.
Thomas Hardy: Behind the Mask. The History Press, 2011.
A Brummie Boy goes to War. Halsgrove, 2011.
Hitler: Dictator or Puppet? Pen & Sword, 2011.
Winston Churchill: Portrait of an Unquiet Mind. Pen & Sword Books, 2012.
Charles Darwin: Destroyer of Myths. Pen & Sword Books, 2013.
Beatrix Potter: Her Inner World. Pen & Sword Books, 2013.
T.E. Lawrence: Tormented Hero. Fonthill, 2014.
Agatha Christie: The Disappearing Novelist. Fonthill, 2014.
Lawrence of Arabia's Clouds Hill. Halsgrove, 2014.
Jane Austen: Love is Like a Rose. Fonthill, 2015.
Kindly Light: The Story of Blind Veterans UK. Fonthill, 2015.
Thomas Hardy at Max Gate: The Latter Years. Halsgrove, 2016.
Corfe Remembered. Halsgrove, 2017.
Thomas Hardy: Bockhampton and Beyond. Halsgrove, 2017.
Mugabe: Monarch of Blood and Tears. Austin Macauley, 2017
Making Sense of Marilyn. Fonthill, 2018.
Hitler's Insanity: A Conspiracy of Silence. Fonthill, 2018.
The Unwitting Fundamentalist. Austin Macauley, 2018.
Robert Mugabe's Lost Jewel of Africa. Fonthill, 2018.
Halsewell: A Shipwreck that Gripped the Nation. Fonthill, 2020.
Beatrix Potter: Her Inner World. Pen & Sword Books, 2020.
The Amazing Story of Lise Meitner: Escaping the Nazis and becoming the World's Greatest Physicist. Pen & Sword Books, 2021.

Author's website https://www.andrew-norman.co.uk

Contents

Introduction 7

1. Packsaddle Cottage, Stratford Road, Hampton Lucy, Wellesbourne, Warwickshire: 8 April 1945: Rachel is Born 8
2. Previous Unrest at Wellesbourne 14
3. Arthur and Joan: A Couple on a Mission! 16
4. New Beginnings in Dorset 19
5. The Jordan Family's Predecessors at Bryanston: 'The Big Red 1' 23
6. Arthur Turns to Communism: Jack Dunman 25
7. Arthur Reveals the Depths of his Feelings 31
8. The Plight of Farm Workers: Origins of the Dorset NUAW; Difficulties also Experienced by the Farmers 33
9. Arthur's Duties as Dorset County NUAW Organizer: His Dedication 35
10. The Bryanston Idyll 41
11. September 1949: Rachel, Aged Four, Commences as a Pupil at Durweston Primary School 43
12. Leisure and Other Activities 47
13. Some Curious Aspects to Rachel's Upbringing! 51
14. September 1956: Rachel Aged Eleven Commences as a Pupil at Blandford Grammar School 54
15. Some Extramural Activities 59
16. The Jordan Family's Visits to Eastern Europe 63
17. Arthur is Frustrated in his Hopes for Rachel 66
18. Arthur Sticks his Neck Out 68
19. Arthur is Dismissed from his Post: Protests 71

20.	Aftermath 75
21.	For Rachel, Hungary Beckons: Marriage: Life Behind the 'Iron Curtain' 78
22.	Rachel's Remarkable Hungarian In-Laws!. 83
23.	Escape!. 91
24.	Life Under the Soviets: Arthur Hears the Truth 93
25.	Joan in Retirement: Rachel Returns to Dorset 96
26.	Rachel and I Meet: Marriage. 99
27.	A Visit to Tolpuddle: Pre-War Commemorations of the Martyrs 102
28.	Arthur's Role in the Rebirth of the Tolpuddle Rallies 109
29.	Other Events Relating to the Martyrs 111
30.	The Post-War Tolpuddle Rallies: Rachel Remembers 113
31.	Where in Tolpuddle did Each of the Martyrs Live, and By Whom Were They Employed? 119
32.	A Visit to Dorchester, Scene of the 'Crime' 124
33.	The Return of the Martyrs. 126
34.	Arthur in Retirement: Education; Books; Steam Trains 128
35.	8 April 2005: Arthur and Rachel are Reunited: I Meet Arthur for the First Time 130

Epilogue 132

Index. 134

Introduction

In April 1946, Arthur Jordan arrived in Dorset from the English Midlands to take up the position of Agricultural Trade Union Organizer for the National Union of Agricultural Workers (NUAW) in that county. In 1948 he was joined by his wife, Joan and infant daughter, Rachel when accommodation had been found for the family in Bryanston, near Blandford Forum in the north of the county. In this idyllic countryside Rachel thrived, not only in her lessons at the local grammar school, including domestic science at which she came top, but she also excelled at her music and her tennis.

Simultaneously, however, there was a parallel narrative going on in her life, because shortly after his arrival in Dorset her father, Arthur became a convinced Communist – a rare phenomenon in those days of the Cold War!

How did Arthur's political views and those of his wife, Joan (who shared them) impact on Rachel? Did she herself embrace Communism? Did she reject it, or was she simply indifferent to it? Did having a father who was a Communist impact negatively on her life in this leafy conservative corner of rural Dorset?

Rachel modestly described herself as an uninteresting person who had an exciting life. But the excitement that was to follow for her was of a nature that neither of her parents could possibly have imagined!

1

Packsaddle Cottage, Stratford Road, Hampton Lucy, Wellesbourne, Warwickshire

8 April 1945: Rachel is Born

The cottage in which Rachel was born was of red brick and it dated from 1836. It was a farmworker's cottage, a tied cottage set in the very heart of the Warwickshire countryside, and 2 miles from the town of Stratford-on-Avon (Stratford), famous for being the birthplace of playwright and poet, William Shakespeare.

Rachel's father, Arthur Ernest Jordan was born on 24 January 1918 at 7 Windsor Street, Stratford-on-Avon, Warwickshire. His father Francis ('Frank') John Jordan, a postman, was serving on the Western Front, as Private Soldier, first in the Royal Warwickshire Regiment and subsequently in the Machine Gun Corps (the First World War having, as yet, almost another year to run). The war ended on 11 November 1918.

Arthur was an only child and his mother, (Ellen) May – 'Nanny Jordan' – was manageress of the refreshment room at Stratford railway station on the Stratford-on-Avon and Midland Junction Railway (SMJ, which became part of the London, Midland and Scottish Railway [LMS] at the amalgamation in 1923). The outcome was that Arthur developed a lifelong love of trains, especially from the golden age of steam. He would also write books about the railways.

Packsaddle Cottage (front), Packsaddle Hill, Hampton Lucy, Warwickshire. Photo: Bob Penrose.

Arthur was educated at Stratford's King Edward VI Grammar School: the very same school that Shakespeare had attended in the 1570s, three and a half centuries earlier. There was no 11-plus entrance examination in those days, and the grammar school was only for those who had the means to pay. In this case, it was May's earnings from her work at the station refreshment room that provided the funds required. However, Arthur described his schoolboy education as 'dreadful' and 'spent the rest of his life trying to secure a decent education'.

Arthur's parents (Ellen) May and Francis ('Frank') Jordan during the First World War.

When he left school, Arthur started work as a booking clerk for the London, Midland & Scottish railway at Stratford Station. He subsequently obtained employment in the West Midlands, working with traction engines. Arthur also became involved in the Stratford branch of the NUAW, a branch which he established in 1943. In the role of Branch Secretary he was extremely successful. In the words of Warwickshire's NUAW organizer, F. Harrison, the outcome was 'that they were now some 10 times as many branches in Warwickshire as in 1939 [and this] was in no small part due to Mr Jordan's efforts, for he travelled many miles and visited many villages in his enthusiasm to organize rural workers'.

The Second World War broke out with the invasion of Poland by the Nazis on 1 September 1939. Arthur described the First World War as 'this terrible and bloody war in which men were killed and maimed believing it to be a war to end war', and which 'saw hundreds of thousands of men leave the land to fight for a land which had treated them so scandalously'. Of the Second World War, Arthur said, 'September 1939 saw our men once again taking up arms to win the peace which our statesmen had so successfully lost between 1919 and 1939'. 'Daddy, to the end of his days, was a committed pacifist who did not believe in war and fighting', said Rachel, 'so, as a conscientious objector, he was sent to work on the land'.

Arthur worked on a large farm in the civil parish of Wellesbourne (a few miles outside Stratford) which was owned by farmer, Clyde Higgs. And this is where he met Joan, his wife-to-be, in October 1942.

(Marjory) Joan Burman was born on 20 March 1921 at 43 Priestley Road, Sparkbrook, Birmingham to parents, John Frederick Burman a dairyman master, and Dora Marjory (née Johnston). Her brother, David was born six years later. Shortly after Joan was born her paternal grandfather, Thomas Burman of Marston Green near Sheldon, Birmingham, bought Fern Farm at Adlestrop in Gloucestershire as a gift for John and Dora. Joan was therefore brought up with horses and ponies.

Horse-drawn carriage outside Stratford-on-Avon Station in 1923, which provided a taxi service to hotels and guest houses. Arthur's mother, May (right), Manageress of the refreshment rooms on right of picture.

When Joan was aged eleven her parents paid for her to attend the grammar school at Chipping Campden, to which she travelled to and fro the 14 miles by train from Adlestrop Station on the so-called 'Cotswold Line'. Not surprisingly, poet and critic Edward Thomas's eponymous poem of 1917 became very dear to her:

Yes, I remember Adlestrop—
The name, because one afternoon
Of heat the express-train drew up there
Unwontedly. It was late June.

The steam hissed. Someone cleared his throat.
No one left and no one came
On the bare platform. What I saw
Was Adlestrop—only the name

And willows, willow-herb, and grass,
And meadowsweet, and haycocks dry,
No whit less still and lonely fair
Than the high cloudlets in the sky.

And for that minute a blackbird sang
Close by, and round him, mistier,
Farther and farther, all the birds
Of Oxfordshire and Gloucestershire.

However, on 8 April 1933, when Joan was just twelve and had been at the grammar school for only just over a year, her mother died aged thirty-seven and Joan was obliged to leave the school. But this was not before she had won a crystal bowl trophy for athletics. She now attended the local state school, as her father was suffering heavy financial losses during the Depression.

Worse followed. As the result of the Great Depression of 1929, John Burman became bankrupt and was forced to sell the farm. He was now desperate for money.

John met a lady called May Clifford who agreed to rescue him financially on condition that he married her. They married in June 1934 and purchased a detached house in Kidderminster in the adjacent county of Worcestershire, where she bought John a milk delivery business.

May was jealous of Joan's relationship with her father, John so she sent her to be brought up by a succession of aunts, sisters of her late mother, 'which she hated!' Meanwhile, her brother David was tolerated and allowed to stay at home. However, he vowed to leave as soon as he reached the age of sixteen, which he did. David subsequently became a successful farmer in Herefordshire. Occasionally, Joan and David were allowed to meet, so they would not lose touch. Joan was finally taken in by her maternal Auntie Mona and her Uncle Billy, a butcher at Yardley, Birmingham and with them she was happy.

Joan on her first pony at Fern Farm, Adlestrop.

Joan's parents John Frederick Burman and Dora Marjory Burman (née Johnston).

'Mummy was glad when war broke out on 1 September 1939', said Rachel, 'because this gave her the opportunity to do something useful with her life. The following day, she rode her bicycle to Lichfield, Staffordshire, and joined the Women's Land Army': she was nineteen years old.

(Marjory) Joan Burman, second from left, in uniform of the Women's Land Army during the Second World War.

Joan and Arthur at Farmer Clyde Higg's farm, where they first met in October 1942.

Arthur and Joan met in October 1942 whilst working for Farmer Clyde Higgs. They were married on 17 January 1944, at All Saints' church, Bromsgrove, Birmingham. 'Neither of them believed in God and neither of them were religious,' said Rachel.

Arthur and Joan were allocated a tied cottage – defined as a property that was occupied subject to the tenant working for its owner. This was Packsaddle Cottage.

Rachel's parents were fit, strong, athletic types. On the farm, said Rachel, 'Daddy and Mummy drove the tractors, Massey Fergusons, grey in colour. They used to put sacks over the tractors' lights at night, to prevent them being spotted by enemy aircraft. Meanwhile, they would hear the drone of German bombers heading for Coventry. At night, some of the workers slept in hammocks slung from the trees.'

'When I was born,' said Rachel, 'Mummy didn't have the money to go to a maternity home, so the midwife called. She was not only horrible, but unhygienic, and the result was that Joan contracted puerperal fever, was admitted to an isolation hospital, and

Joan and Rachel (aged six months).

PACKSADDLE COTTAGE, STRATFORD ROAD, HAMPTON LUCY, WELLESBOURNE, WARWICKSHIRE: 8 APRIL 1945: RACHEL IS BORN

Alison Rachel Jordan, Birth Certificate, 8 April 1945.

nearly died. I guess that was why she never had any more children.'

Prior to 1847, countless women who were attended by midwives after giving birth died of this fever, which had a mortality rate of between 70% and 80%. But after the work of Hungarian physician and scientist Dr Ignaz Semmelweis in that year, this disease should have been confined to the history books. Semmelweis insisted that nurses washed their hands in a solution of chlorine prior to undertaking the delivery of babies and gynaecological examinations. Whereupon the rates of puerperal fever at his hospital dropped virtually to zero. And yet, when Rachel was born just under a century later, this lesson had still not been learned! The infection is now known to be caused by the streptococcal bacteria.

Christmas 1947. Rachel (aged two years eight months) at the Bancroft, Stratford-on-Avon (her birthplace).

2

Previous Unrest at Wellesbourne

Early trade unions were created with the onset of the industrial revolution in about 1760, and by 1825, they were widespread in London.

According to lifelong socialist and historian of the labour movement, Reginald Groves 'The story of the farm workers' first national trade union begins in the small village of Barford, Warwickshire, on the cold, wet morning of 12 February 1872. On that morning two or three men called at the cottage of 46-year-old agricultural labourer and Methodist lay preacher, Joseph Arch.'

Two days later, on 14 February 1872, there was a gathering of over a thousand disaffected farmworkers. The meeting was advertised secretly, by word of mouth, and that evening, under lantern light, Arch addressed the labourers. The outcome was that 'some 200 or 300 put their names down for [i.e. to join] the union that night'.

A dissertation by Arthur, written in 1943 and entitled 'The Growth of the National Union of Agricultural Workers', indicates that he was well aware of the significance to trade unionism of Joseph Arch, and of the village of Wellesbourne, Warwickshire in the district where he and Joan lived and where Rachel was born. Of the members of the crowd that Arch addressed, said Arthur, who were demanding a wage of 12 shillings per week, few of them could have dreamed that the national wage would one day rise to 70 shillings per week'.

On the following Wednesday, 21 February 'there was another even larger meeting under the Wellesbourne chestnut tree'. Whereupon 'a committee was formed, and a secretary appointed to organize the union'.

On the afternoon of Good Friday, 29 March 1872, 'the Wellesbourne committee held a conference, and here the decisions were made that brought the Wellesbourne union and the many village unions into one society – the Warwickshire Agricultural Labourers Union.' Its objectives were to achieve an increase in wages and a decrease in working hours for the farm labourers of the county: 'to improve their habitations; to provide them with gardens or allotments; and to assist deserving and suitable labourers to migrate and emigrate.'

Arch also provided the impetus for the creation of the National Agricultural Labourers Union a month later in May 1872, with himself as its president. But despite the union's initial success, falling membership and a series of unsuccessful strike actions led to it being dissolved in 1896.

In 1906, the National Union of Agricultural Workers was established as the Eastern Counties Agricultural Labourers and Small Holders Union (ECALSHU). In 1910 its name was changed to the National Agricultural Labourers and Rural Workers Union (NALRWU). In 1920 it became the National Union of Agricultural Workers (NUAW). (In 1968, the NUAW became the National Union of Agricultural and Allied Workers.)

3

Arthur and Joan
A Couple on a Mission!

'Because of what Daddy had witnessed as a young man in rural Warwickshire,' said Rachel, 'he felt that the farm workers had a bad lot in life, and he made his feelings known. This resulted in him being sacked by Farmer Higgs, just after I was born.'

Arthur's only 'crime' had been to try and persuade his fellow workers to join the union – a perfectly legal and legitimate activity. He and his new wife and their baby daughter were now evicted from their tied cottage.

Arthur had become a victim of precisely what he was attempting to protect his fellow workers from, and henceforth, abolishing the tied cottage system became a central plank of his mission as a trade unionist.

So, what did the Jordans do? 'We had no choice but to go to Daddy's parents, Nanny Jordan and her husband, Frank in Stratford. That was in July 1945.' Did Rachel have any recollection of those times? 'As a toddler I have only fleeting memories,' she said. 'Nanny looked after me during the day because Mummy had a job doing a milk round. I remember Nanny Jordan making me a dummy, as you couldn't get proper ones. She wrapped some sugar in a piece of muslin for me to suck on. Mother was annoyed, but she couldn't stop Nanny doing it!'

'I remember helping Grandpa Jordan to shell peas in the garden behind the coal shed. There was a long garden path at the side of which he placed a row of inverted jam jars to make an edging. Grandpa Jordan used to take me in my pram and pushchair to the Bancroft, where he used to push me on the swing,' she continued. The Bancroft was a delightful park, on the opposite side of the River Avon to the town of Stratford and the famous Shakespeare Memorial Theatre (renamed the Royal Shakespeare Theatre in 1961).

'One day there was a thunderstorm, and I was so frightened, I cried!' Another memory of Rachel's was seeing Morris dancers in the square outside the Stratford Memorial Theatre. 'I also remember being in the Bancroft with "Peggy", Grandpa and Nanny Jordan's dog'. Dogs would become an important part of Rachel's life, and she would always speak of her pet dog with great affection.

In 1943, Arthur wrote, 'What of the Future? If we go forward, and we shall go forward, then the National Union of Agricultural Workers will be playing its part to the full in building a new Britain, a prosperous agricultural industry, and assisting the men and women of the land to live a full life.' He also envisaged a time when NUAW members would sit in the House of Commons as MPs.

The Second World War ended on 2 September 1945 with the unconditional surrender of Japan.

Arthur was not idle for long, and he applied for the position of Dorset County Organizer for the NUAW (which also included forestry workers). Having been required to write a detailed account of his activities as NUAW Branch Secretary at Stratford, he was called for interview at NUAW headquarters in London. He was successful, and shortly afterwards received the following letter from the NUAW General Secretary Alfred ('Alf') Dann, dated 1 April 1946:

'The Executive Committee were in agreement with your commencing work in Dorset for the Union as Organizer from 8th April next, at a salary of £6 per week. The car mileage rate we pay from your home to any distance on Union work is 3½d per mile, and we pay 50 per cent of complete insurance to cover car.' The NUAW also loaned Arthur the money to buy a car, his job being dependent on his having one. Arthur was now twenty-eight years of age.

However, 'it was nearly three years before we were found somewhere in Dorset to live,' said Rachel, 'so Mummy and I remained in Stratford and Daddy found digs at "The Laurels", Winterbourne Kingston near Bere Regis in Dorset. Finally, we were offered a place to live in Bryanston, near Blandford Forum (Blandford), and in December 1948 Mummy and I moved south, and the family was reunited.' Dorset, in southern England of course, is where the legendary 'Tolpuddle Martyrs' were born and bred!

The so-called Tolpuddle Martyrs were six agricultural labourers from the eponymous Dorset village, who had been instrumental in founding a trade union in October 1833 namely, 'The Tolpuddle Lodge of the Friendly Society of Agricultural Labourers'. Their employers had reduced their wages from nine shillings to seven shillings per week, which was a mere half of what was needed to provide the bare necessities of life for one single agricultural labourer, let alone for him or herself and his family to subsist on. In the words of their intellectual leader, George Loveless, this was an attempt by the men to save themselves from 'utter degradation and starvation'.

The Tolpuddle men were successful, and some 40 or more labourers enrolled in the first few weeks. The act of founding a trade union was not, in itself, illegal. In fact, several trade unions were already in existence at the time. However, the Tolpuddle unionists had sought advice from a London trade union which had insisted that prospective members of the Tolpuddle Union must swear an oath of loyalty to the union. This action was illegal, and it was the grounds for the six men, who were considered to be the ringleaders, to be brought to trial.

The six men were arrested at dawn on Monday 24 February 1834 and taken to His Majesty's Gaol, Dorchester to be tried at the next assizes. They were George Loveless aged thirty-seven, married to Elizabeth (née Snook) and with three young children; James Loveless aged twenty-five, George's brother, married to Sarah (née Daniel) with two children; Thomas Standfield aged forty-four, married to Dianne (née Loveless), George and James's sister with six children; John Standfield aged twenty-one, Thomas's son, unmarried; James Hammett aged twenty-two, married to Harriet (née Gibbons) with one child; James Brine aged twenty, unmarried. (Hammett was the only one of the six with a criminal record, having been imprisoned in 1829 for allegedly stealing some pieces of iron.)

It took the jurymen only about five minutes to find all the prisoners guilty, and on the morning of 17 March 1834 the judge, Mr Baron Williams, addressed them:

'I am bound to pronounce on you the sentence which the Act of Parliament has imposed. I therefore adjudge that you, and each of you, be transported to such places beyond the seas as His Majesty's Council in their discretion shall see fit for the term of seven years.'

The six men were now clapped in irons and transported, as convicts, to penal colonies overseas. George Loveless was transported to Van Diemen's Land (now called Tasmania): an island off the coast of south-eastern Australia. The other five men were transported to the Australian mainland. Conditions were harsh, and many who were transported in this way died of malnutrition, disease, or ill treatment at the hands of their masters. All the six Martyrs, however, survived.

4
New Beginnings in Dorset

The new abode of the Jordan family at Bryanston was a modest building, one of four which were universally referred to as 'The Huts', set back 50 yards or so from the tarmacked road, know to the locals as 'The Drive' and located on the edge of woods. The land had previously belonged to the Portman Estate. In those days, the only other sign of human habitation in this region were a handful of similar huts scattered throughout the woods and six Portman Estate cottages at the side of The Drive.

The only access to the hut was on foot, by way of a short path the width of only a single flagstone, with thick foliage on either side. 'The postal address was Number 8 The Cliff, Bryanston', said Rachel, 'and I remember that its wooden front door was painted green. This would be our home for the next six years.'

The huts comprised a block of three concrete ones in front and a larger single one behind which was wooden. All four huts had flush toilets (since they were inhabited by US Army officers, as will shortly be seen) when even the occupants of the Portman Estate cottages had to rely on a row of privies, located across the yard at the rear. These elegant, brick-built and slate-roofed cottages had been built for the workers of the eponymous estate.

The front block of huts each had two bedrooms. The right hand one, as seen from The Drive, was occupied by the Dunford family: father, John ('Johnnie'), and mother, Ellen who was expecting her first baby, Ann, who would grow up to become Rachel's lifelong friend. The middle hut was occupied by Peg and Maurice Coombes who had two boys. 'Peg made my ice-skating dress and all my ballet dresses,' said Rachel. The left-hand hut was occupied by Ivor and Betty Dominey who had two girls and a boy. 'My bedroom and our kitchen window faced Ann's bedroom and the back bedroom window of the Coombes next door. Between us was a quadrangle full of stinging nettles!'

'Our hut had three bedrooms,' said Rachel, 'whereas the others had only two. One of the bedrooms served as Daddy's NUAW office. Each day his secretary, Miss Bartlett, came all the way (some 5 or 6 miles) from Winterborne Kingston on the bus and walked up from Bryanston Lodge, then cut through the woods at the back of our hut.'

'We always kept a couple of goldfish in a plain glass tank. Nobody bothered about chlorine in the water in those days and they were fine. Mummy cleaned the tank weekly.'

Around the huts, an area had been cleared for the residents to grow their vegetables. 'In those days, even after a hard day of physical work, manual workers went out into the garden to tend their vegetables and flowers. On the opposite side of the road was a large shed, formerly used by the US military, which Daddy rented to garage his car. In those days, Daddy was the only person in the village who owned a car, apart from the squire, of course!'

'Daddy smoked cigarettes but changed to a pipe when I was about seven. I loved the smell of the burning tobacco. First, he had a curly one, and then a straight one, like Prime Minister Harold Wilson. He gave up smoking before I was aged ten but Mummy, who had smoked since the age of nineteen when she joined the Women's Land Army, continued!'

'My mother, Joan as a housewife, had the task of coping with running the home. There were no machines in those days and life was physically demanding. On Mondays she boiled up the copper to do the washing, stirred it, pulled it out with the tongs, carried it outside, put it through the mangle, and hung it on the line. Then she emptied the copper. No wonder Monday's meal was cold meat left over from the Sunday roast as there was no time for cooking that day. On Tuesday it was ironing, and the clothes had to be aired.'

'Once a week on a Friday, Ken Morse from the co-op grocery store in Blandford arrived in a brown overall with a pencil behind his ear. He would sit down and take the order from Mummy for everything we needed. Grocers did not sell bread, so the baker used to stop his van on The Drive and carry his big wicker basket down the path to our four huts. He got to know, more or less, what each family would have.'

Did Rachel have lots of kisses and cuddles? 'From Daddy, yes. He was always cuddling me and lifting me up on his shoulders. But Mummy, no. She was not the cuddling type. I think this was because when her mother died, and her stepmother had sent her away, she never experienced hugs. But she was always caring and giving. She gave me everything. I was lucky. I had a very happy childhood.' Surely Rachel's own loving and caring nature derived from the love she had received from both parents, expressed in their two different ways.

Did Rachel's parents ever criticise or scold her? Did she ever get a 'telling off'? 'No, they didn't criticise me, but of course I got told off!' On one occasion, just before November 5th – 'Bonfire Night' – Rachel was

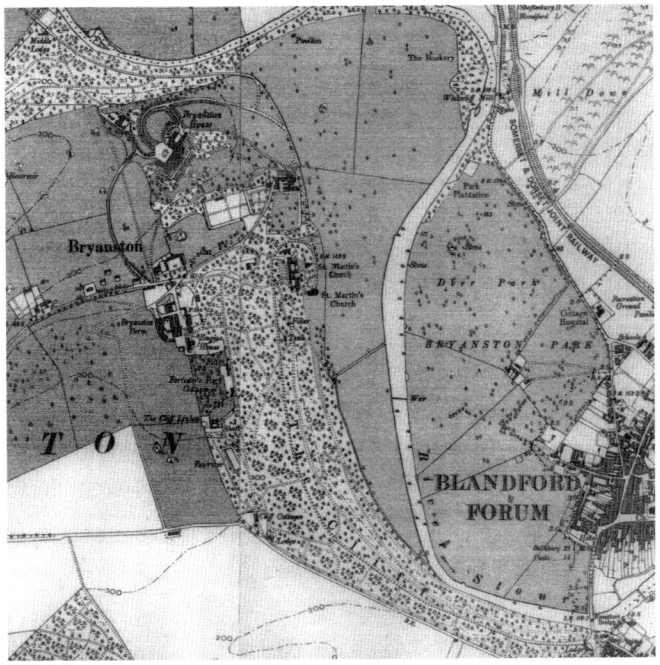

Bryanston to Blandford Forum, 1.2 miles. Ordnance Survey, 1901.

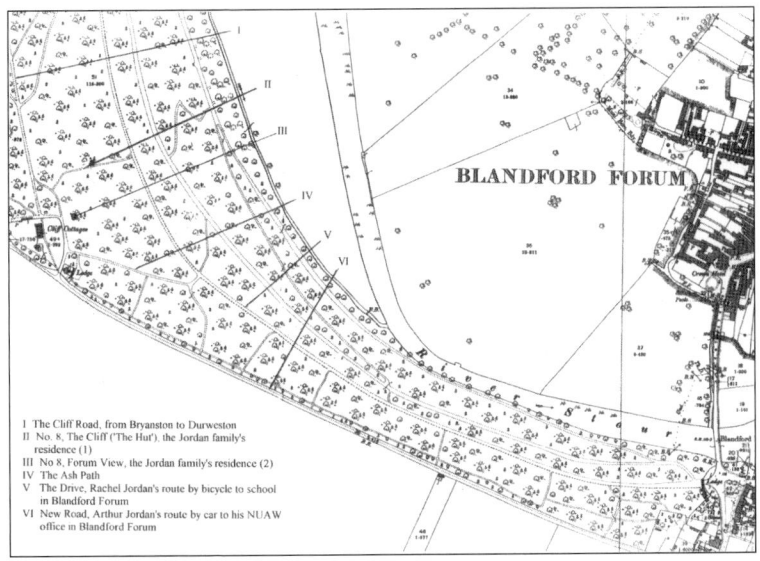

I   The Cliff Road, from Bryanston to Durweston
II No 8, The Cliff ('The Hut'), the Jordan family's residence (1)
III No 8, Forum View, the Jordan family's residence (2)
IV The Ash Path
V   The Drive, Rachel Jordan's route by bicycle to school in Blandford Forum
VI New Road, Arthur Jordan's route by car to his NUAW office in Blandford Forum

uncharacteristically rude to her mother. This resulted in her being ordered to her room, so she missed the fireworks and the bonfire, which she could doubtless hear, and see her little friends enjoying from her bedroom window. So yes, this was a loving household, but there were rules and boundaries, as on that rare occasion, little Rachel learned to her cost! 'Joan and Arthur didn't believe in "smacking", so punishments were always for me to "miss out" on something I was looking forward to!'

From the huts, turn left onto the road called 'The Cliff'. Then turn left again onto the Ash Path which leads through the woods. Then turn right onto The Drive, which was bordered with sweet-smelling mock orange (*philadelphus*) bushes. The Drive led to Bryanston Lodge, entrance to the Portman Estate. Having passed through the lodge gates a left turn into West Street brings the traveller to Blandford Bridge over the River Stour, the Crown Hotel, and Blandford's Market Place. The total distance travelled is about 1¼ miles.

Alternatively, from the Ash Path, turn right and The Drive leads to Bryanston School, a distance of a mile or so. The school was formerly a private house, the home of the Portman family. In those days Bryanston School, which was independent and for fee-paying pupils, was for boys only. Their school uniform was light grey wool-worsted shorts, grey jumpers, and ¾ length woollen socks. 'Every Thursday, the VI Form boys were allowed to walk into town, and we often passed them on The Drive.'

Take a right turn from the huts and follow the road for a good half mile down the steep hill into Bryanston village. In those days, the village consisted of a farm; buildings housing farm equipment with living quarters above; farm labourers' cottages with outside toilets; a blacksmith's forge, and a tiny village shop. All the buildings were of red brick, apart from the farmhouse which was of Portland stone.

Meanwhile, on 12 January 1951 Arthur's father Frank Jordan died suddenly at the age of sixty-five in the entrance drive to Stratford's train station, having succumbed to a severe heart attack. His widow, May, died seven years later in 1958.

5

The Jordan Family's Predecessors at Bryanston
'The Big Red 1'

Prior to the occupation of 'The Huts' by the Jordan family and others, larger feet than Rachel's had trod the tracks and lanes of Bryanston: feet whose owners had come from across the Atlantic Ocean to help save Europe from the scourge of Nazism.

John Tory, Blandford Town Museum's President, had, like his father, Philip before him, been tenant of the Home Farm at Bryanston and he remembered Arthur well. John provided the following information about the US soldiers who had occupied the huts during the Second World War. They were members of the US 1st Infantry Division, nicknamed 'The Big

Insignia of the US 1st Infantry Division, carved into the brickwork of the Old Stables, Bryanston, presumably by a US GI in 1944 or 1945. Photo: Alan Shrimpton.

Red 1' (after their shoulder badge on which the number '1' is depicted in the colour red).

The division arrived in Liverpool on 7 October 1943, after participating in the Sicily Campaign. A contingent of about 300 men from the division arrived in Bryanston on 9 October 1943 for intensive training in preparation for the D-Day landings, specialising in inactivating gun positions.

Division Headquarters was located at Langton House, a Georgian mansion a mile or so to the east of Blandford, the commanding officer being Major General Clarence R. Huebner. 1st Division Signal Company, commanded by Major Leonard Peters, was located at Bryanston Camp, and it was the major who probably previously occupied the Jordans' hut.

It was ironic, therefore, that Arthur, a pacifist, and a conscientious objector, should have succeeded the US Army major as occupant of 'Number 8 The Cliff, Bryanston'.

As 6 June 1944 – 'D-Day' – loomed, the 1st Infantry Division comprised 34,142 men and 3306 vehicles.

'In Bryanston Camp the white soldiers were billeted in huts on either side of the road along The Cliff at Bryanston. The huts were located in the woods so as not to be seen by passing enemy aircraft. The black soldiers were billeted in the Old Stables by the church (down in the village). The woods, where Rachel and her little friends were subsequently to play as children, gave cover to the buildings, tents, vehicles (including tanks) and supplies.'

On 3 June 1944, Bryanston suddenly became deserted as all the men and vehicles moved to Portland. Before the US 1st Infantry Division left, one of the GIs carved the Division's insignia, the number '1', into the brickwork of the Old Stables.

On 6 June 1944 the Division landed on 'Omaha Beach', Normandy where, after great loss of life, they broke through the German lines and led the spearhead through France; then on through Belgium, to Germany on 10th November.'

'Over the D-Day campaign 1,973 of the Big Reds were killed and 11,448 wounded, 951 were reported missing and 631 were captured in total.'

When the Second World War ended in 1945, the wartime Bryanston Camp was largely demolished, but 10 or so huts were left for the local housing authority to provide much needed homes for local people – and also for the Jordan family!

6

Arthur Turns to Communism
Jack Dunman

In 1946, the year following Arthur's arrival in Dorset to take up the post of County Organizer for the NUAW, he met John ('Jack') Dunman, a staunch Communist whose influence would set him on a new path.

'I remember Jack Dunman well', said Rachel. 'He was a most impressive fellow. A lovely, big burly man, public school educated and very well spoken.'

Jack was born on 5 February 1911 in Poole, Dorset. He was, therefore, almost seven years older than Arthur. Jack's father, Percy was a timber merchant and married to Lisa (née Griffin). Both were Methodists.

Jack, their only son, won a scholarship from the local grammar school to a public school, Marlborough College. From there he went up to Balliol College, Oxford to study philosophy, politics, and economics. Jack joined the Labour Party in 1929.

Whilst at Oxford, said Jack's daughter, Jessica her father 'read Marx for the first time and developed a lasting interest in left-wing politics'. [Karl Heinrich Marx (1818-1883), German philosopher, ecomomist, and social revolutionary whose works inspired the founding of many communist regimes in the twentieth century.] Jack also 'helped found the socialist rural journal, *The Country Standard: For Peace and Socialism in the Countryside*, and he remained its editor throughout his life. Farming was always Jack's main interest, and he was an active member of the Agricultural Workers' Union'. However, in February 1933, Jack changed his allegiance and joined the Communist Party.

Jack met his wife-to-be Helen Muspratt in early summer 1936. Said Jessica 'When Jack met Helen he was working as a traffic apprentice for the London and North-East Railway in Cambridge'. He had chosen to work for the railways 'in order to gain experience in industry'. So, railways were also something that Jack and Arthur had in common.

Helen was born in Madras, India on 13 May 1907. Her father was an Indian army officer who served in the First World War. By 1921 the family had been reunited in England and set up home in Swanage on the Dorset Coast. Helen studied photography at Regent Street Polytechnic in

London. In 1928 she set up a photographic studio in her hometown.

In 1932, Helen met fellow photographer Lettice Ramsay who was on holiday in Dorset. In that same year, they opened a photographic studio together in Cambridge. Said Jessica, 'Lettice was very popular in left-wing intellectual circles and there were lots of parties at the studio. She introduced Helen to her friends, who included Guy Burgess, Donald Maclean, and Anthony Blunt.' All three of these men were photographed by Helen and Lettice in their Cambridge studio. In fact, they were all spies for the Soviet Union (full name, Union of Soviet Socialist Republics, or USSR).

Helen (née Muspratt) with husband, Jack Dunman and children: Mark, Kate, and Jessica. Photo by Joan Muspratt. Courtesy Jessica Sutcliffe.

In 1936, Helen joined the Communist Party. In summer that year, she 'set off for a six-week trip to the Soviet Union to see socialism in action.' Here, she filmed farmers and villagers in the vicinity of the Volga River.

On 25 March 1937, Helen and Jack were married. He was now working in the industrial department at Communist Party Headquarters, King Street, Covent Garden, London, with special responsibility for agricultural workers.

In summer 1937, Helen visited South Wales and photographed the miners and unemployed labourers of the Rhondda Valley. Said Jessica, 'This direct experience of waste, poverty, and unemployment had a strong effect on her and helped to reinforce her socialist views.'

'With their growing commitment to the ideals of communism, Jack and Helen soon made a momentous decision about their future life together. Jack would give up his career with the railways and take up a poorly paid job with the Communist Party.' Meanwhile, 'Helen threw her political energies into the Campaign for Nuclear Disarmament'.

In 1940, the second year of the Second World War, Jack sustained a severe head injury, which exempted him from military service.

It was soon after the Second World War that Arthur met Jack Dunman, who was to change his life for ever. At the time, Jack was Chairman of the Berkshire and Oxfordshire NUAW and living in Harwell in Berkshire.

'Helen's parents lived at Cliff Cottage on the seafront at Swanage', said Rachel, 'and in the summer holidays, Jack and Helen used to visit them with their three children. Daddy used to drive Mummy and me down from Blandford and we used to meet with them, and relax on the lawn, go for a swim, or take long walks around Arne and Studland.'

'Like Daddy, Jack loved children,' said Rachel. 'Daddy's motto was: "Children are the future. That's why you have to cherish them". On these walks Daddy would engage in earnest discussions with Jack, whilst Helen and my mother, Joan walked behind with Helen and Jack's daughters Jessica and Kate, and I brought up the rear.' This is where the seeds of Communism were sown in Arthur's mind.

Jack wrote several pamphlets for the Communist Party which Arthur would, undoubtedly, have read. They included 'Farmworkers for Peace and Higher Wages' (1950); 'Food and Farming' (1963); and 'Co-ops: The Future' (1969). The policy of the Communist Party, he said, 'is based on the belief that agriculture must provide:

1. Good wages, conditions, and security for the farmworkers.
2. A good standard of living and security for the farmers.
3. Plentiful good and cheap food for the consumers.'

He also declared that the tied cottage 'should be abolished'. This was also an ambition fervently shared by Arthur. Furthermore, 'a substantial part of the land should be brought into public ownership by nationalising the land of the large landowners but without disturbing the small owners and owner-occupiers. The Communist Party's proposals are all based on the fact that the fight for a prosperous and expanding agriculture is part of the fight against monopoly capitalism: a fight in which only the working-class movement can take the lead.'

Jack also extolled the virtues of the cooperative, and its belief that industries and commercial concerns should be owned and controlled by the people working for them, for their joint economic benefit. The movement exists, said Jack, 'to supply its members with reliable goods at the lowest prices consistent with good conditions for its workers'.

Jack, like Arthur, had witnessed at first hand the plight of agricultural workers, and both were engaged on a mission to improve their lot. For example, he calculated the essential living expenses of a typical farmworker's wife: in this case a Mrs Vant of Kent. They amounted to £4 11s. 8½d. per week, which she said, 'leaves 2s. 3d., out of which my husband has to buy his smokes and a pint if he is lucky'.

Arthur had become disillusioned with the Labour Party and with Socialism which, he believed, were incapable of achieving this end, but now, through the influence of Jack, he saw Communism as the way forward. The outcome was that Arthur joined the Communist Party of Great Britain. Joan also joined the Party, even though she came from a wealthy farming family.

In fact, Arthur described himself as a Marxist. So, how are Socialism, Communism and Marxism defined? According to the *Oxford Dictionary*, Socialism is defined as:

'A political and economic theory of social organization which advocates that the means of production, distribution, and exchange should be owned by the community as a whole.'

And Communism is defined as:

'A theory or system of social organization in which all property is owned by the community and each person contributes and receives according to their ability and needs.'

As for Marxism, it is defined in the *Chambers Dictionary of World History* thus:

'Marxism contends that capitalist societies are subject to crises which create the conditions for proletarian revolutions and the transformation to socialism. Because of private capital's need to earn profits or extract surplus value, wages have to be kept to a subsistence minimum. This produces economic contradictions, because it restricts the purchasing power of workers to consume the goods produced. Capitalism is, therefore, inherently unstable, being subject to crises of booms and slumps. Marx's view was that these crises would become increasingly worse, and eventually lead to revolution, whereby the working class would seize the state and establish a dictatorship of the proletariat, productive power would be in public hands and class differences would disappear. This classless society would eventually lead to the withering away of the state, producing a communist society'.

In other words, in Marxist theory, as the *Oxford Dictionary of English* states, 'Socialism is a transitional social state between the overthrow of capitalism and the realization of Communism'. This explains why in the West, the Soviets were described as Communists, whereas they describe themselves as Socialists. However, said Hungarian History Professor István Petrovics:

'The Communist Party of the Soviet Union (CPSU), first of all under Lenin's leadership and then under Stalin's, reinterpreted Marxist ideology as Marxism-Leninism-Stalinism, a major feature of which came to be democratic centralism. Unlike the spontaneous, decentralised organisation envisaged my Marx, the CPSU was a highly centralised, monolithic, and secretive organization. Under Stalin's leadership it became an instrument in the development of a totalitarian dictatorship.'

Polish historian Isaac Deutscher summarized the position perfectly. Stalin, he said:

'...saw to it the anti-Communists should be squeezed out of the governments of eastern Europe and suppressed. He installed the single-party system all over the Soviet sphere of influence. And he sent out his plenipotentiaries, administrative experts, generals, and police agents to instruct and supervise the local Communist parties and governments, and to impose on them a single policy and a single discipline'.

However, 'increasingly from the 1960s onwards' said Petrovics:

'...the compulsory leadership of the CPSU was questioned and challenged, partly because of the economic difficulties resulting from the rigidities of democratic centralism in industrial states, where decentralisation and flexibility were required.'

'I myself would be a Marxist,' said Rachel. 'Anyone would if they read Marx and Engels.' This was a reference to German political philosopher and economist, Karl Marx, and German socialist and political philosopher, Friedrich Engels. 'But it's idealistic,' Rachel continued. 'Life isn't like that! Both these young men, Daddy and Jack, were living in an idealistic world. Then you realise, it doesn't work!'

Also, there was one aspect of Marxism that neither Rachel nor her father, Arthur would have condoned, and that was that Marx (and Engels) believed in violence to achieve the revolutionary overthrow of capitalism by the proletariat. In 1848, Marx wrote chillingly:

'There is only one way in which the murderous death agonies of the old society and the bloody birth throes of the new society can be shortened, simplified and concentrated, and that way is revolutionary terror.'

Similarly, in 1849, Engels declared:

'The next world war will result in the disappearance from the face of the earth not only of reactionary classes and dynasties, but also of entire reactionary peoples. And that, too, is a step forward.'

Trade Unionist and Communist, Graham Stevenson in the *Country Standard*, described Arthur as a 'capable organizer', not only for the NUAW but for the Communist Party (CP) also. Arthur had served 'for a period of twelve years on the [Communist] Party's Executive Committee [Governing Body]'. Whereas locally, he had established 'a branch of 13 [CP members]' in Blandford in 1950, and in 1956 the CP 'had finally established monthly meetings in Dorset'.

However, in his efforts to boost membership of the Communist Party in Dorset, Arthur was to be sadly disappointed, as he himself admitted in April 1958 in the Communist Party's *World News & Views*. 'Over the years', he said:

'We have had successes and failures but whilst we cannot claim to have increased the size of the party in Dorset, or to have established the party as a political force, we do feel proud that these comrades, isolated as they are, should have remained steadfast during the recent difficult period.'

This was a reference to the brutal suppression in Hungary of a national uprising by Soviet tanks and troops on 4 November 1956. Thousands were killed and wounded and nearly a quarter of a million Hungarians fled the country. After this catastrophic event, Dorset lost four of its NUAW members, who resigned in protest.

In her book, *Joan Maynard: Passionate Socialist*, educationist, Professor Kristine Mason O'Connor stated that Jack Dunman, 'a Communist Party member and Union activist, had warned Arthur Jordan against saying he was representing the Union when making political speeches or attending political events.' She quoted Dennis Hodsdon, who became Assistant Secretary of the NUAW, as saying that in the 1960s, 'There was a real fight in the Trade Union Movement to prevent Communists and hard left taking absolute control. The majority of the membership did not want that.'

(The Trade Union Movement, which was legalised in 1871, sought to reform socio-economic conditions for working men in British industries.) One day, Arthur would have cause to remember Jack's warning!

Jack Dunman's final work, *Agriculture: Capitalist and Socialist*, was published in 1975, the draft copy of the manuscript having been delivered to the publisher only a few days before his death on 30 October 1972.

Rachel had the fondest memories of Jack. 'One day we were at Shell Bay, Studland with the Dunmans when my beach ball blew into the sea. It was a rubber ball – this was before the age of plastic – and quite expensive. "Don't worry," said Jack, who was a strong swimmer. "I'll soon get it back for you." But alas, the wind was too strong. I was heartbroken.'

'Another day, when we were at Ringstead Bay near Weymouth, we saw a man in a wooden rowing boat waving frantically to us from out in the bay. (We were the only people on the beach.) The boat was sinking. Daddy and Jack immediately swam out and rescued him. It turned out that the bung had become dislodged, and the boat had filled with water. Furthermore, the man could not swim!'

7

Arthur Reveals the Depths of his Feelings

In July 1947, an article by Arthur entitled 'Socialism in Whose Time' was published in the *Dorset Standard*, price one penny. In it, he revealed, perhaps more than in any of his other speeches or publications, the depths of his hatred of the capitalist system and of his exasperation with the Labour Party. Arthur described how, in the Soviet Union 'where they have Socialism', farmworkers and miners were offered holidays in beautiful hotels situated in beautiful health resorts. 'One third of them are getting their holiday FREE. For the rest, up to two-thirds of the cost is born by the state social insurance fund.'

By contrast, in the English south coast resorts of Bournemouth and Eastbourne, for example, the hotels were 'choc-full of people who have never worked and are not wanting in spite of it. These hotels are full of people who hate Socialism', and 'who do everything possible to wreck the Labour Government.'

'What I am trying to show you, comrade, is that although we have a Labour Government which, make no mistake, has achieved a great deal for the workers, they are not moving towards Socialism fast enough. They are not gaining the confidence of the workers. They are pandering to the capitalists too much, and we have got to stop them.'

'As land workers we demand control of all food prices so that our wage increases can be real. We demand less food for the expensive hotels and restaurants and more for the farmworkers' kitchen table and the local canteens. More houses in the villages and fewer additional bedrooms and bathrooms to mansions. We demand freedom for farmworkers and their families at once. End the tied cottage system now and don't let's have excuses from the Labour Government. We demand workers' control of the industry; the land should be nationalised before anything else, for land ownership is the basis of the capitalist system and that is what we are out to smash, isn't it? Workers on the land must demand Socialism now, in our time.'

'This month in Dorset we celebrate the victory which the Tolpuddle Martyrs won over oppression in 1834 but let us not forget that the battle is still on. All that we have won can be very easily lost if we are not determined in our efforts to build a socialist state in which all men work and all enjoy the fruits of their labours.'

This was a reference to the aforementioned legendary six agricultural workers from Tolpuddle, Dorset who, in their efforts to create a trade union in 1834, had been cruelly victimised by the authorities.

8

The Plight of Farm Workers
Origins of the Dorset NUAW; Difficulties also Experienced by the Farmers

The suffering and hardships endured by farm labourers were described by Jack Dunman and witnessed by Arthur as a young man, working on a farm in rural Warwickshire during the Second World War, and subsequently in rural Dorsetshire. This experience would inform Arthur's thinking for the remainder of his life.

In September 1917, at the instigation of James ('Jimmy) Lunnon, the National Agricultural Labourers and Rural Workers Union (NALRWU)'s National Organiser, Tom Higdon undertook a speaking tour of Dorset. Lunnon was born into poverty in London in 1869. Higdon, son of an agricultural labourer, was also born into poverty in East Pennard, Somerset, in that same year. Higdon's wife Annie (née Schollick) was a schoolteacher.

Annie was appointed headmistress of a school in Norfolk, with Tom as assistant master. However, the couple had been threatened with dismissal from this school, and they were actually dismissed from their next school for complaining about the inhumane conditions under which the pupils were being taught. Meanwhile, in 1907, Higdon became branch secretary of the Eastern Counties Agricultural Labourers and Small Holders Union (ECALSHU). The outcome was that the trade unions rallied round, and with donations received, the Higdons built as an alternative, the Burston Strike School in the eponymous Norfolk village.

As a result of Higdon's visit, the Dorchester & District branch of the National Agricultural Labourers and Rural Workers Union (NALRWU, successor to the ECALSHU) was established in September 1917. Fred James, son of a Dorset shepherd, was its first branch secretary.

Shortly afterwards, a meeting of NALRWU members was held at Bugler's Café, Dorchester and addressed by both Lunnon and James.

The inaugural meeting of the Dorset branch of the NALRWU branch was held at the Dorchester Corn exchange on 29 November 1917. It was chaired by the Reverend C. W. Lloyd-Evans, Vicar of Milborne St Andrew.

At this time, the NALRWU had 134 members in total. Most of the local branches of the NUAW in Dorset were established in that year.

It should not be forgotten, however, that the life of a farmer could also be precarious. Philip Tory became a tenant of Home Farm, Bryanston in 1951. His son, John described how the land on which the farm stands was once part of the Portman Estate, but had since come into the possession of the Crown.

'In the early 1820s, the Portman family owned lands in Dorset which included not only Bryanston but also most, if not all of Durweston, Pimperne, Stourpaine, Shillingstone, Child Okeford and Hammoon, plus part of Blandford with extensive woodlands and about 10,000 acres of farmland. The family also owned estates in Somerset & Devon, and valuable land in the Marylebone area of London.'

'But their luck ran out as the introduction of death duty in the 1890s and vast increases in the levels charged (set by David Lloyd George, Prime Minister of the United Kingdom 1916-1922, to pay for World War I) hit the Portmans very hard with three Lord Portmans dying in the 1920s and three more in the 1940s, the last of these in 1948. This led to the government taking Bryanston and Durweston in lieu of duty and they became part of the Crown Estate.'

'Private estates had always selected tenants as they wished but the Crown being a governmental body had to fall in with its rules and Home Farm, Bryanston was let by open tender. In 1951 my father's bid of £3 per acre per year was accepted, and he was granted security of tenure, but only for himself and not for any widow or offspring that he may have had.' However, Philip's son, John was fortunate because in 1969, he applied for and was granted the tenancy of Home Farm by the Crown Estate in succession to his father.

9

Arthur's Duties as Dorset County NUAW Organizer
His Dedication

Arthur's NUAW office was located down a small alleyway (now called Georgian Passage) leading off Blandford's East Street. The postal address was 61 East Street and the telephone number, Blandford Forum 155. In one room were two desks, one for Arthur and one for his secretary, Mrs Welch. A communicating door led to another room which housed a Gestetner duplicating machine, with one wall covered by an enormous Ordnance Survey map showing every single settlement and every NUAW branch in Dorset. Said Rachel:

'Daddy wore a check tweed, light brown and dark brown jacket, cavalry twill trousers, and fine leather shoes from Hobbs' men's outfitters in Blandford. He only ever had one suit, and that was the one he was

Arthur Ernest Jordan.

married in. It was navy blue with a very fine grey stripe, and he wore it all through my childhood. I remember the NUAW badge that my father always wore in his lapel. On it was depicted a ploughman and two shire horses pulling the plough'. Badges for long service carried a bar, with the number '10', '25', or even '50' denoting the length of the owner's memberships in years.

Arthur's duties included attending the meetings of the Dorset County NUAW Committee which were held every three months or so at NUAW headquarters in Dorchester, and of the Dorset NUAW Branch Committees, of which there were in excess of 100, which were held quarterly.

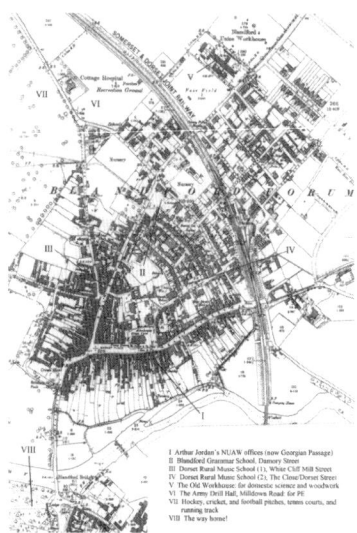

Blandford Forum, Street Plan. Ordnance Survey, 1900.

Arthur attended his first NUAW County Committee meeting at Dorchester on Saturday 13 April 1946, with H. M. Haward as president and W. Palmer, as county secretary. The 'Tolpuddle Celebrations' for the following year, 1947, were discussed, and Arthur stated that these would commence on 20 June. The NUAW's Executive Committee, he said, had decided that 'Tolpuddle Sunday' was to be 'a national event', with the celebrations spread 'over a period of days. The Executive Committee, together with all the union's organisers, would spend the week in Dorset with conference and special meetings. Trade Unionists from all over the county would be welcomed'.

On a personal note, Arthur said that 'he recalled the traditions of the Dorset branch of the union dating back to the Tolpuddle Martyrs,' and he also recalled with pride, the day when, as a visitor, he had stood in the dock that those very six men had occupied in 1934.

Arthur ended by paying tribute to his predecessor as the NUAW's District Organizer for Dorset Fred James, former alderman and Mayor of Dorchester, whom he greatly admired, 'saying that he once heard the branch referred to as the "Freddie James Union"!'

Reading between the lines, it was Arthur, as NUAW County Organizer and a passionate devotee of the Tolpuddle Martyrs, who was determined

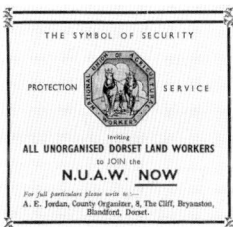

An invitation to join the NUAW, 1949.

to ensure that the annual 'Commemoration' in their honour, which Fred James had started in 1922, would be reinstated after the war.

In addition to his NUAW commitments, Arthur was also Secretary of Blandford Trades Council. The function of Trades Union Councils, often referred to simply as Trades Councils, is to promote effective solidarity in disputes, joint campaigns on issues such as health, education, welfare, and transport, and, in general, provide the vital link between the workplace and the wider working-class community.

Scrutiny of surviving minutes of the above meetings reveals that Arthur was present at almost every single one. He was involved in the production and presentation of committee reports, including financial reports; discussions about ways of increasing the wages of the agricultural workers and obtaining a reduction in their working hours; the provision of NUAW Weekend Schools; farm safety; bus services; the boycott of South African goods during these years of apartheid; securing improvements to the government pension service for the farm labourers, and the provision of washing facilities for them on the farms; the proper recording of accidents that took place on the farms.

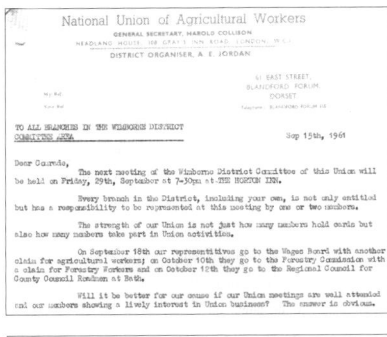

Letter from Arthur Jordan, Dorset County Organiser, to all branches in the Wimborne Committee Area, dated 15 September 1961. This contained an analysis by him of attendances at the seven branches of the Wimborne District Committee and ended with an exhortation to branches to improve their attendance records!

From 1910, the NALRWU had begun to accept not only farm workers but also roadmen – men employed to repair and maintain the roads – carters, gardeners, navvies, and women. The indefatigable Arthur served as NUAW representative at meetings of the South-western Regional Council for County Council Roadmen, held in the Guildhall, Bath, Somerset every three months.

Arthur also visited the homes of sick or injured members of the NUAW, asessed their needs and, if necessary, represented them at industrial tribunals when, for example, they were in danger of being thrown out of their tied cottages. 'I remember when George Andrews of Milborne St Andrew broke his back in an accident on the farm and he became bedridden,' said Rachel. 'Daddy visited him several times and went to a tribunal to try and get him compensation. Daddy spent a great deal of his time at such tribunals, arguing the case for those who had fallen ill or been injured, and were being forced out of their tied cottages on that account. He usually won his case, and they got their money.' Sadly, George lived for only a few weeks, having contracted pneumonia. 'When a member of the NUAW died,' said Rachel, 'Daddy always made a point of attending the funeral, as in the case with George.'

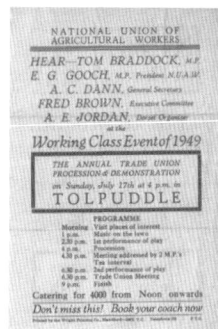

'Daddy was an extremely hard-working man,' said Rachel. 'In addition, he organized the annual outings of the Dorset Branch of the NUAW, and Mummy and I always accompanied him. This was a day which everybody looked forward to. Twelve coaches gathered up the members from the villages and this took several hours. There was a stop at mid-morning for a toilet break and an opportunity to stretch the limbs. Then Daddy checked that everyone was back on board the coaches. Daddy had pre-arranged parking for the coaches, at whichever place we went to, for example Plymouth.'

'Everybody convened in a ballroom or dance hall as it had to be large enough for several hundred people or more to sit down to a hot lunch. After that, everyone was free to do what they wanted. This was a day of freedom and relaxation. The coaches left for home at 5 p.m., stopping at a pub on the way back so the men could get their beer. There were sing songs on the coach, and everyone always thoroughly enjoyed the day.'

In fact, the annual outings which Arthur organized attracted from 700 to 1200 members. 'Daddy also organized union dinners, which generally drew 250 or so people.' As for Joan, said Rachel, 'At union events or at festive events in aid of the union, it was always Mummy and two or three other wives who made the teas and refreshments. They also organized a market stall at Christmas time in Blandford to sell food, toys, and clothes. Daddy could not have done what he did without my mother in the background. It was her support that kept everything going all through the years!'

Finally, from the early 1950s, the NUAW held an annual May Day rally in Dorchester in which Arthur, as NUAW County Organizer, was also heavily involved.

In 1952, Jess Waterman, County Chairman of the NUAW, stated that 'during the seven years they had Mr Jordan as County Organizer, Dorset had become the third best organized area in the country.' In the same year, it was reported that the union 'represented 90% of all agricultural labourers in the County of Dorset. Moreover, Jordan had secured improved pay for Dorset roadmen and sought to improve their status.' It was reported that 'his tireless efforts ensured the remarkable achievement of 100% union membership in the [Dorset] villages of Sutton Waldron, Fontmell Magna, and Tarrant Hinton.' And an article in *Land and Labour* stated that only the counties of Norfolk, Lincolnshire, and Dorset could win comparably high membership of the union, and even then, it went no higher than 80-90%.

On 21 December 1957 it was unanimously agreed by the Dorset County NUAW Committee that 'Sister Joan Jordan' (Arthur's wife) be nominated to represent the NUAW at the forthcoming Women's Trade Union Congress. This indicates Joan's commitment to the union.

In 1958, Arthur himself reported that over 200 roadmen, or one third of the total employed, were members of the NUAW.

On 27 February 1960 'Bro. [Brother] Jordan quoted figures showing that there were some 3874 members [of the NUAW] in Dorset and that Branch Income for 1959 had totalled £7275. 283 new members were enrolled during 1959'. 'Brother' and 'Sister' were the common forms of address by members of the unions.

Annual outing for Dorset NUAW members organised by Arthur. (Arthur second from left, then NUAW President Edwin Gooch, then the Mayor of Plymouth.)

A decade earlier, on 5 October 1950, at a meeting of the Shaftesbury and Gillingham Committee, 'Bro. Jordan referred to the position of the union nationally in which there was some considerable fall in membership, and whilst this was mainly due to the large number of workers leaving agriculture – 14,000 since last year – it had to be emphasised that only an increased membership of the union could ensure that there would be no falling back in living standards.' In Dorset, Arthur would strive might and main to achieve this end.

On 6 October 1960, again at a meeting of the Shaftesbury and Gillingham Committee, 'Bro. Jordan reported on the negotiations for the increase in the agricultural minimum wage. He said that the 9/- [nine shillings] increase was largely the result of the agitation carried on in a number of counties, including Dorset.'

In that year of 1960, Arthur organized a visit of NUAW members to South Wales to 'Deep Duffryn mine, Mountain Ash, then a Communist stronghold. He reprised the trick for a visit to the Standard Motor Company, whose convenor was the legendary communist, Bill Warman in order that town could understand countryside, and vice versa.' Arthur also 'arranged a day trip of 800 union members to the Forest of Dean'.

On 2 June 1961, 'Bro. Jordan reported to the Wimborne District Committee on the Union's [NUAW] approach to the government to secure some protection for the occupants of tied cottages.' This was a subject close to his heart; his own family having been previously evicted from their tied cottage. 'A deputation of Union members had been to see the Minister of Housing and had submitted a very comprehensive report on our experience of the tied-cottage system in agriculture, together with our proposals for avoiding evictions.'

In that year, Arthur organized another visit to South Wales, to the coal mines and the National Union of Mineworkers. By now the Dorset NUAW had over 4000 members.

On 5 December 1962, under the heading 'County Roadmen', to the same committee, 'Bro. Jordan reported [to the Shaftesbury and Gillingham Committee] on the wage claim, zoning [the designation of roads for a particular purpose], method study, and the issue of duffel coats.'

In that same month of December 1962, at a meeting of the Dorset County NUAW Committee, 'Brother Jordan produced figures for the estimated cost of sending a delegation to Poland'.

10

The Bryanston Idyll

Arthur described Dorset as the loveliest county in England. He, Joan, and Rachel had holidayed in Cornwall and Devon and elsewhere, but it was the small fields the abundant hedges and hedgerows, the undulating country, the woodlands, the thatched cottages, and the heaths which gave Dorset its unique charm. True, there were beautiful places on the Devon and Cornish coast, but Arthur found the stone walls that surrounded the fields of those counties somewhat cold and unfriendly.

Anyone arriving in Bryanston, Dorset in the late 1940s and the area known as 'The Cliff' to the south-west of Blandford would have thought themselves in a rural paradise. The Cliff rises high above the River Stour with farmland to the south. This was an intensely wooded area with all the beautiful indigenous English trees: beech; birch, oak, horse chestnut, sycamore. There were also birds a plenty: blackbirds, chaffinches, thrushes, all singing their hearts out from morn till night, as the occasional kestrel threatened from overhead, and squirrels scampered up and down the trees. Native plants included: wild garlic, cowslips, primroses, bluebells, anemones, granny bonnets, dandelions, daisies. This was a little piece of old and unspoilt England; an idyllic environment for Rachel to have experienced in her childhood, and during our courting days she told me about it in glowing terms. At Bryanston, she said, 'May was a lovely time of year. The April showers had come and gone; now came the sun.'

'Every Thursday or Friday, hops were brewed by the local world-famous Hall & Woodhouse Brewery, located to the south of Blandford Bridge, and the smell filled the air as we walked down The Drive.'

Milk came from Farmer Philip Tory's Home Farm in the village of Bryanston, located about a mile away down a steep hill. 'My best friend, Mavis Lane's father, Albert was the head dairyman at the farm. His horse pulled the cart with its two churns of fresh milk up the hill. Whereupon everyone would go out with their can, and he would ladle out a measure from the churn.'

'Mummy would push me into town in my green-coloured canvas pushchair, often in company with Ann's mother, Ellen. They would walk down the ash path and onto The Drive to Bryanston Lodge gates, then over Blandford Bridge and the River Stour. Sometimes Mummy would allow me to walk along the entire length of the parapet of the bridge as she held my hand. I well remember the metal sign when I learnt to read. It said that anyone who damaged the bridge would be transported which meant being clapped in irons and shipped to Australia. Mummy would then call at the butcher and Macfisheries, the fishmongers. Finally, they began the long walk home again. Buses were only twice a week in those days.'

11

September 1949
Rachel, Aged Four, Commences as a Pupil at Durweston Primary School

Rachel's journey from Number 8 The Cliff to Durweston Primary School, some 3½ miles to the north-west, involved her walking along the flagstone track to where bus driver, Mr Barnes stopped at regular intervals to gather up his little charges. 'The school bus was green in colour. On each side, below the windows, was a long leather-covered wooden bench, and in the middle at the back was another bench where the older children (in the top class) sat. When the bus negotiated a sharp bend, they frequently rolled off!'

Eight children lived in the huts in the woods and two in the Portman cottages. On schooldays, if someone was not present at their usual pick-up point, the bus driver simply waited, and the mother might come out and say, 'Little Johnny won't be coming to school today'. In Bryanston village it picked up another eight or nine children.

The bus had commenced its journey at The Kennels, Winterborne Stickland and travelled to Bryanston village along the tarmacked road through the Portman Estate following alongside the River Stour far below, past Middle Lodge and into Durweston. After dropping the children off at the school it turned

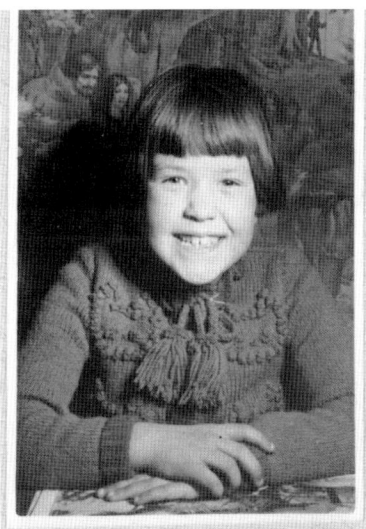

Rachel (aged eight) at Durweston Primary School.

right and then over Durweston Bridge and right again onto the main road into Blandford.

'One winter, the snow lay so thickly on the ground that the school bus to Durweston could not get through, so two of our teachers walked all the pupils from Bryanston home!'

At primary school, a 'dinner' was provided at lunchtime but no glass of water. In fact the only liquid that the children had during the school day was the ⅓ of a pint bottle of milk at morning break.

Every day we pupils were required to attend a service at Durweston's church of St Nicholas.

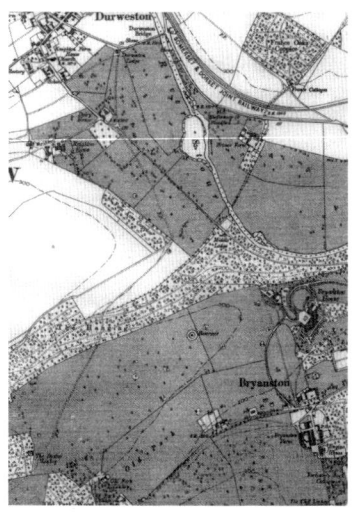

Bryanston to Durweston, 3.4 miles. Ordnance Survey, 1901.

And every Friday, between 9 a.m. and 11 a.m., the vicar came to hear the top class recite the catechism, 'which we learned by rote, even though we hadn't got a clue what it meant'.

'On Shrove Tuesday each year, the whole school (around 50 or 60 in all) would call at every house in the village and sing 'Here we come a Shroving', as the teachers made a collection for Dr Barnardos. Ours was the only school in Dorset to maintain this tradition.'

'In my final year at Durweston School I was voted the 'May Queen', with two "Matrons of Honour". We also danced round the maypole, weaving in and out, the object being to plait the ribbons round the pole in an attractive pattern.'

'In my time, the front of the school was laid to lawn with flower beds, and this is where we performed handstands and roly-polys. Next to the school was a large field in which we children played rounders and cricket, and all the Sports Day events took place here.'

Adjacent to the school, and almost as large, was Mrs Brooks', the headmistress's house. She was a war widow, and she lived alone. Rachel frequently suffered from earache. Whereupon the kindly Mrs Brooks would take her into her house and tuck her up in bed. 'She was a dear lady', said Rachel. 'When she retired, she went to live with her daughter in Bournemouth, but she kept in touch and even sent me postage stamps for my birthday.'

Rachel (centre, aged ten) as 'May Queen', Durweston Primary School, with her two matrons of honour.

Mr Albert ('Bertie') Unwin joined the school a year or so prior to the retirement of Mrs Brooks and he succeeded her as head. He was 'a super guy who got us pupils interested in Vivian Fuchs's expedition to the Antarctic. In 1958, the English explorer and his expedition completed the first overland crossing of Antarctica.'

When she was at primary school, did Rachel ever make little presents for her parents? 'We learnt to do "feather stitching"', she said, 'and I made Mummy a case for her sewing needles.'

Rachel would sometimes 'go with Daddy to visit the agricultural workers in their cottages. In that way I got to know the name of just about every single village in Dorset. "Purse Caundle"; "Winterborne Zelston"; "Huish Episcopi". Wonderful names! Names to conjure with! Daddy's car was a Ford Consul, registration number 'GTK 591'. The letters and numbers, which were embossed, were made of chromium. I remember the number plate because I used to polish it!'

'The Ford Consul had a bench seat at the front, and a gear lever off the steering wheel. I would sit in the passenger seat, but if he had a colleague with him, I would sit between them in the middle. I would remain in the car whilst he did his visits, which sometimes took over an hour, but I was never bored.'

Rachel often accompanied her father to local Labour Club halls, which he hired in order to show films to the members of the Agricultural Workers' Union, about Soviet state farms and co-operative farms, and how well the workers were looked after, and what benefits they received. She also remembered Chinese films featuring Chinese Communist Revolutionary leader, Mao Zedong. 'All of it was propaganda, in a way,' said Rachel. She also attended jumble sales with her parents in order to raise money for the union.

'The announcement was made that all the huts in Bryanston, including ours, were to be demolished. Twenty-four council houses were built further down on the south side of The Cliff and workmen arrived to clear the trees. Whereupon, all the occupants of the huts relocated to their new homes, the address being 'Forum View'. Our house was 'Number 8'. On the day of the move, our neighbour (Ann Dunford's father, Johnny) arrived at our hut with a large, hand-pulled army trolley and all our possessions were loaded up and wheeled along the road to our new home. The process was then repeated for all the other hut occupants.'

'I was aged ten when we moved into the council house, and it was shortly afterwards that I got my first puppy, "Jipp" – or "Jippy", named after Dora Spenlow's dog in Charles Dickens's novel, *David Copperfield*, though in the novel, "Jipp" is spelt with one "p". My Jipp was a cross between a Jack Russell terrier and a Sealyham terrier. Other pets were two rabbits, each with their own hutch, and a tortoise called "Shelley"!'

'We were living at Forum View when I took my "Eleven-plus"examination, and I remember Daddy running up the stairs to tell me I had passed for the grammar school. I didn't know what all the fuss was about.' In fact, only two pupils in Rachel's school year passed the examination, after which she, and all but one of her other friends, were obliged to go their separate ways.

12
Leisure and Other Activities

'At weekends, weather permitting, we spent all our time outdoors,' said Rachel, 'climbing trees, picking flowers, playing hopscotch, jacks, etc. Every large estate in Dorset was surrounded by iron railings and we used to swing on these for hours. We never worried that somebody unpleasant might be lurking in the woods. We made tracks by trampling down the vegetation, but those tracks must all be grown over by now. Ann Dunford, our neighbour's daughter, and I loved treading in the cows' "pancakes" (cowpats) as we made our way (the short cut!) across the fields from The Cliff down to Bryanston village.'

'On their birthday, every child had a party to which the local children were invited, and I was no exception. When it was my birthday, ten of us sat round the table and ate paste sandwiches, jelly, blancmange, and cakes. Afterwards, we had a film show. Using the 16 mm projector and screen that he used for his union meetings, Daddy would host the occasion, using the big roll of film that he had ordered. Favourite films were of Charlie Chaplin, but I have to say that even in those days I didn't laugh at him much. But one little girl was in stitches the whole time. To watch a film was a novelty, it was a big thing for the children. Then we played musical parcels or musical chairs.'

'There were not many toys to play with in those days, so my friends and I got our mothers to

Rachel (aged five) in the back garden of Number 8, The Cliff, Bryanston, 'with my swing at edge of woods where we lived in an ex-army hut!'. She is wearing a silver wrist bangle, given to her by her paternal grandmother, Nanny Jordan.

lend us some unopened tins of spam, baked beans, tinned fruit, etcetera from the larder and we pretended to be shopkeepers. When Daddy saw what we were doing he said he had a better idea. He took the *Farmer & Stockbreeder* periodical which contained lots of pictures of prize bulls, pigs, and sheep, and he said I should cut out the pictures, stick them onto some cardboard with glue, and invite my friends round, to view them for the fee of one penny each.' I said to Rachel that perhaps, deep down, Arthur was really a capitalist at heart, and she laughed!

'When I was seven or eight, our little "gang" of four or five made its way to the River Stour where we would often see rowing eights pass by, rowed by the boys of Bryanston School. We would climb down the steep bank with our jam jars and try to catch minnows at the water's edge (no adult supervision, even though none of us could swim!). One day, Tony Coombes fell in, and he would have drowned, but his father, Maurice just happened to be there fishing and pulled him out. He was very lucky!'

Arthur, Rachel (aged five), and Joan with her box camera in Cardiff, the castle in background, at a Welsh miners' NUM rally.

'Sometimes, after school, I would cycle down to my best friend, Mavis Lane's house. Mavis's father Albert was head dairyman at Tory's farm. Mavis and I would play together and have jam sandwiches for our tea on the lawn. We used to take Mavis on holiday with us. Daddy was lovely with children. He always found time to stop and talk to them and play. The Lanes had six children (five girls and a boy). Four of the girls went to the grammar school.'

'Every fortnight Mummy and I would go to Bournemouth on the green Hants & Dorset service bus, and I would go ice skating. We would arrive back in Blandford at around 7 p.m. and in wintertime face a long walk home in the dark. This is why we always carried a torch with us.'

Rachel (aged five), at Number 8, The Cliff, Bryanston in 1950. *Rachel and Arthur on the beach at Weymouth, summer 1951.*

A photograph of Rachel shows her as a six-year-old in 1951 on the Promenade at Weymouth, marching with her mother, Joan in the NUAW procession. She was carrying a banner bearing the somewhat ambiguous slogan: 'Restore School Cuts: We are Only Young Once'. 'Daddy wrote the slogans for the banners for people to carry. He would have been at the head of the rally with the NUAW representative from the London head office. Note that all the men are wearing either caps or trilbies.'

'In 1952' said Rachel, 'when I was aged only seven, I carried a red flag at an NUAW rally at Weymouth.' The red flag was a symbol of socialist revolution. Rachel was then only a little girl and too young, she said, to understand the implications of these events.

Similarly, when Rachel as a seven-year-old visited the Old Crown Court in Dorchester with her parents and stood in the very dock from which the Tolpuddle Martyrs had heard their sentence read out, it meant 'Nothing. It didn't mean anything.' But having grown up and come to realise it's significance, she had nothing but loathing and contempt for wealthy Dorset squire and magistrate James Frampton – who spied on the Martyrs, plotted against them, and was chiefly responsible for their conviction – and his ilk!

On 23 June 1955, Arthur wrote to General Secretary Collinson to request that the sum of £10 be deducted from his July salary and forwarded to him as his wife, Joan was due to travel abroad for a month on 1 July and 'she will require some money to travel with'. The request was denied, but Collinson did assist Arthur by sending him a cheque for £10 as an advance payment on his expenses.

NUAW Rally, The Promenade, Weymouth, 1951. Rachel (aged six): 'Me at front with banner saying 'Restore School Cuts: We are Only Young Once",' Joan on her right. 'Daddy would have been at the head of the rally'.

This indicates just how fragile the financial affairs of the Jordan family were, despite them living relatively frugal lives. It also indicates how generous they were to Rachel, providing her with, in addition to the mandatory grammar school uniform and other items required for her schooling, a bicycle with which to get there, her tennis outfit and racquet, private music lessons, trips to classical music concerts, etc.

Rachel (aged seven) and New Forest Pony.

13

Some Curious Aspects to Rachel's Upbringing!

In many ways, Rachel's upbringing could not have been more normal. She had loving parents, playmates all around her, and a freedom to roam that many modern children would envy. But that was not the end of the story!

'Daddy used to ask me, "Why don't you ask more questions? Why aren't you more inquisitive?"' A question that Arthur asked himself was, why does society assume that boys and girls should be brought up differently?

Gender is defined as the state of being male or female, typically with reference to social and cultural differences rather than biological ones. Arthur and Joan believed that girls only played with dolls because they were given them at an early age. Rachel was given soft toys, not dolls, to put in her dolls' pram. Instead of a walkie-talkie doll for Christmas she was given a train set and the following year a Meccano set. At this, she was both bemused and hugely disappointed. The train, 'just went round and round on its oval track. It was stupid!' As for the Meccano set, 'Daddy helped me to make a crane with it!'

Said Rachel, 'I longed for dollies, like other little girls. So, I used to go to my little friend Ann's hut, next door, to play with her dolls! When I was eight, I was eventually given a doll, but it was a black one. I had never seen a black doll, either before or since. But, Daddy's attitude was why should all dolls be white? But by then my friends and I had grown out of playing with dolls anyway!'

As for her attire, said Rachel, 'Mummy dressed me very nicely but ALWAYS in blues or yellow dresses, NEVER pink! On cold winter days I wore dungarees to school. None of the other girls wore dungarees.'

Did Rachel's parents take her on holiday? 'Yes, and I was usually allowed to bring one of my little friends with me. But until I was aged seven or eight, I had to wear a horrible pair of boys' swimming trunks, maroon in colour with a motif of three white monkeys. So, I was bare from the waist up. Whereas Ann had a beautiful, bright orange, ruched little girl's swimsuit. On one or two occasions, when we went to Weymouth, I was allowed to borrow Ann's swimming costume, which fitted me even though I was three years older, because it was stretchy.'

'Daddy used to wait for the tide to come in. Then he would dig a trench leading down to the water's edge. Meanwhile, I would run down to the sea and fill my metal bucket with seawater, to pour into the trench, when it would run back down again. I remember the colour of the bucket. It was yellow.'

A photograph in black and white, taken by Rachel's mother Joan, depicts this very scene. The joy on the faces of the two participants is wondrous to behold. Here was a little child, safe in the bosom of her loving parents, and not only that, having fun! If only life could stand still!

'One day, on the beach at Weymouth I wandered down to the water and got lost. I came out but I couldn't see Mummy and Daddy and I started to cry. A lady came over to comfort me, and then Mummy came. In those days there was a white hut for lost children to be taken to. The beach got so crowded. There were also flying boats moored in Weymouth Bay.'

'When I was fifteen, I went to stay with an aunt in Stratford. She sat me down at her dressing table and taught me how to use make-up. So, when I returned home I was wearing bright red lipstick.' What did her father say when he saw her? 'He was utterly revolted!' said Rachel.

Rachel was given an expensive leather briefcase when she started at the grammar school, when all the other pupils had satchels. I think this was partly because Mummy and Daddy thought the briefcase would fit better on my bicycle carrier.

What kind of toys were children given in the Soviet Union? Today, websites advertising children's toys from the Soviet era indicate that on the one hand, there were there were toys for girls, such as dolls made of plastic and rubber, Russian female folk dancers, ballerinas, an electric toy food mixer, and rubber rabbits which squeaked when you squeezed them; and on the other hand, there were toys for boys, such as military vehicles – for example, a military tank and three-man crew complete with firearms, and toy guns. Finally, a battery-operated record player, a pinball game, a remote-control space exploration vehicle, and a steerable pedal car might have appealed to both boys and girls equally. 'When Daddy arrived in the GDR [East Germany] in the late 1950s he was very surprised to see that little boys were playing with toy guns.'

Rachel remembered watching two Soviet films in particular, having been present when Arthur showed them to his NUAW colleagues. 'The Cranes are Flying' 1957, (in black and white) is a romance concerning a Soviet couple whose lives are torn apart by the Second World War. In fact, the heroine Veronika's boyfriend, Boris is killed in that war. However, before Boris goes off to war there are tender love scenes. And as for Veronica, attired as she is in a pretty blouse with puffed sleeves and pinafore dress with broach, with her wavy hair worn shoulder length, or tied up in a bun, she is the epitome of feminine beauty.

The second film, 'And Quiet Flows the Don' (in colour), was also released in 1957. It was based on the novel by Mikhail Sholokhov and describes the life of the Don Cossacks during the First World War, the Russian Revolution, and the Russian Civil War. Here, the women again appear feminine, with pretty dresses, blouses, and tunics, and use make-up and wear earrings, even when they are conducting menial tasks such as fetching water in buckets from the river!

14

September 1956
Rachel Aged Eleven Commences as a Pupil at Blandford Grammar School

In September 1956, at the age of eleven, Rachel commenced at Blandford Grammar School, a co-educational school situated at the top of the hill at the junction of Salisbury Street and Damory Street. The school's motto was 'Non Sine Pulvere Palma' – 'No Reward Without Effort'.

'Three hundred and twenty or so pupils attended the school,' said Rachel: 'the ratio of boys to girls being dependent on how many had passed the 11 Plus Examination. Lessons were mixed and we were only segregated for PE and games and at breaktimes.'

'There were ten male members of staff and eight females. When I began there, the headmaster was Mr Hughes. A year later he retired and was succeeded by Mr Jones. The headmistress was Miss Dakin. Pupils came to the school from the surrounding villages: some from Spetisbury on the local bus; others by train from Shillingstone and Sturminster Newton.' Rachel used to cycle the 2 miles or so to school from her home, Number 8 Forum View. 'If the weather was very bad, then Daddy gave me a lift to school.'

The journey to school began along what the locals called the 'Ash Path', which ran for about 30 yards and on which they tipped ash from their fires to counteract the mud, down the long drive to Bryanston Lodge; across Blandford Bridge, past the Crown Hotel, into the Market Place, and up Salisbury Street to the top of the hill. 'This was quite a feat with a heavy briefcase on my rear carrier.'

'In those days everybody walked or cycled. There was no ferrying around of children in motor cars. This was simply because only very few people could afford them. And although Daddy did have a car, he was out most evenings on union business. But on rainy days, Daddy would take me to school, and at the end of the school day I would walk down the hill and meet him at his NUAW office.'

'In the summer, after the school day, I would come home and have my tea; get changed and cycle all the way back to the games field for tennis

SEPTEMBER 1956: RACHEL AGED ELEVEN COMMENCES AS A PUPIL AT BLANDFORD GRAMMAR SCHOOL

Blandford Grammar School: War Memorial Arch. Left to right: Wooden hut on brick foundation with 3 or 4 steps where Latin and RE were taught; building where First Formers (IA and IB) had their desks (formerly cowsheds). Pupils moved around to appropriate classrooms depending on the subject of their lessons; through arch on rhs library (formerly stables); main building; entrance to corridor leading to VI Form room and female staff room. Photo: Christopher Hazlewood.

practice!' Who had taught Rachel to play tennis, at which she would excel? 'That was Daddy,' she said. 'I would get home at about 8 p.m., and then start doing my homework and practising with my violin.'

Entrance to the grammar school was via the Memorial Arch, which was inaugurated on 3 June 1925. The Arch bears the names of 18 former staff and pupils of Blandford Secondary School (precursor to the grammar school) who died in the First World War, and of 17 former staff and pupils of Blandford Grammar School who died in the Second World War. 'That is all that remains of my old school,' said Rachel. She now described the layout of the school.

'On the right-hand side, beyond the Memorial Arch, all the buildings were of brick construction. Enter via the porch and there were three choices. Turn right, and a door led into the school assembly hall. Here, at morning assembly, all the teachers stood on a raised platform wearing their black gowns, the head with his lectern. Go forward a couple of steps and here was the female staffroom. Or, from the entrance porch turn left into the tiny VIth Formers' room, where they could make their own coffee or tea. Just past this room there was a corridor on the left which led to the taller main building.

On the ground floor of the main building was the men's staffroom. On the first floor were the headmaster's and headmistress's study, and on the second floor lived Mr Joyce the janitor and his wife. The front door to the building was strictly out of bounds for staff and pupils. This was Mr and Mrs Joyce's private entrance. Mr Joyce was also the groundsman for the playing fields, situated opposite the Cottage Hospital. Here were lovely grass tennis courts, cricket, football and hockey pitches, a running track, and a nice wooden pavilion for changing. The fields stretched right down to the banks of the River Stour. Beyond the main building was the library, which our teacher told us had formerly been stables. It had its original semi-circular windows on the first floor, where the stable boys lived, and great double green doors, the entrance being large enough to admit a horse and carriage. The library also served as the debating room, or as a venue for the school orchestra, of which I was a member, to practice at lunchtime.'

'The first building to be encountered on the left-hand side, having passed through the Memorial Arch, was a wooden hut where Latin and R.E. (Religious Education) were taught. Beyond this were two brick-built classrooms where the First Formers (IA and IB) had their desks. These, so our teacher told us, had formerly been cowsheds! There were several other classrooms dotted around the site, all of them prefabs, including the chemistry and physics laboratories. So, horses and cows once had the luxury of brick-built accommodation, whereas human beings now occupied wooden huts!'

Blandford Grammar School had started life as Milldown School in 1863. In 1903 it became Blandford County Secondary School, and in 1927 it became the town's grammar school. However, from the age of the brickwork and internal fireplaces, it is clear that the school was not purpose built, and that it had once been a private house (possibly a farm) of which only the stables and the cowsheds had survived.

'As there was insufficient space in the grounds,' said Rachel, 'we went to outlying places for some of our lessons. For example, domestic science and woodwork were taught in the old workhouse at the top of Salisbury Road. For Physical Education – "PE" - we walked with our teachers to the Army Drill Hall which was on the way to the Cottage Hospital. This was equipped with climbing ropes, horses, a springboard, etc. This had to be timed so that we got back to school for the next lesson. For PE and games lessons boys and girls were taught separately.'

A photograph of Rachel in the school library shows her studying a magazine with three of her female schoolmates. But, she said, 'I was never really interested in books. In fact, I don't know why I was at the grammar school. I think it was a prestigious thing for the parents, that's all.'

Rachel recalled that although the grammar school had flush toilets, 'they were located outside, behind the biology lab. But there were no handwashing facilities, unless one walked back across the yard to the girls' cloakrooms,

The library, Blandford Grammar School, 1961. (Left to right) Jenny; Georgie; Rachel; Vicky.

which nobody ever did! But no one ever got an upset tummy. Neither was there a source of drinking water. Furthermore, no free bottle of milk was provided, as had been the case at primary school. And when we went out to play at weekends, none of us were given drinks to take with us. Looking back now that is the reason why I was always constipated, and why I lived on syrup of figs and Ex-lax chocolate and other laxatives. I was simply dehydrated.'

Rachel (aged seventeen) in grammar school uniform, taken by her boyfriend, Nigel.

At primary school, the fact that her father, Arthur was a Communist did not affect Rachel adversely in any way. However, now she was at the grammar school, that was to change.

'The discrimination against me on account of my father being a Communist wasn't so much by the children,' she said, 'but by some of the teachers. However, it was done surreptitiously, not to my face. For example, no mention was ever made of the fact that I had performed in concerts with my violin; played with the National Youth Orchestra; and won many trophies for tennis. Instead, the only privilege I was allowed was to captain the tennis 1st VI. Anyone else would have been recognised for what they did for the school. However, I wasn't. I was not even made a prefect, when generally in the Upper VIth you would expect to be. Anyone else would certainly have had a mention.'

The irony of it was that Rachel had no more interest in Communism than her teachers. 'There were 16 pupils in our sixth form,' she said. 'We had a debating society and Daddy expected me to speak out for the rights of people. However, I never wanted to have an opinion on anything, and I never said anything if I could help it. I just hated it all. I was apolitical.' However, some of her teachers had neither the wit nor the desire to see that the situation was not of Rachel's making, and instead, they decided to 'take it out on her' in underhand ways.

To be fair to her parents, said Rachel, 'they did not sit down with me and try to indoctrinate me. They just took me along with them'. Did Rachel's parents acknowledge her successes and reward her for her achievements. 'Of course! They bought me an LP that I wanted, and regularly took me to concerts at Bournemouth's Winter Gardens because they knew I loved classical music.'

Rachel: 'Me, Vicky, Alex, Diane. We still made it to school in deep snow!' Bryanston, winter 1962.

Rachel in the VI Form at Blandford Grammar School, struggling through a physics lesson!

Blandford Grammar School VIth Form, 1963. Rachel: 'There were only 16 of us. My boyfriend, Nigel took the photo. Front left: me, Diane, Vicky. Immediately behind me: Georgie, my best friend, who actually made my wedding dress!'

15

Some Extramural Activities

From the age of thirteen, Rachel had excelled at tennis, won the school tennis trophy every year, and subsequently became captain of the girls' first team. Who had taught her to play tennis, at which she would excel? 'That was Daddy', she said.

Rachel: 'My first tennis trophy won when I was aged eleven!'

Rachel had also excelled at music. 'My parents took me every fortnight from the age of seven to the Winter Gardens in Bournemouth to hear the Bournemouth Symphony Orchestra. The cheapest tickets were half a crown, and this was for the rows which were actually on the stage but behind the orchestra. Here, the acoustics were not of the best, but from here I had the best few of all the musicians and their instruments. During one performance the conductor Charles Groves (that was before he was made a "Sir"), picked me out and said to the audience "This little girl comes here often". Whereupon they gave me a clap. I had plaits then. Another conductor who I greatly admired was the young Italian Pierino Gamba.'

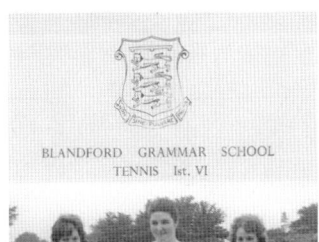

'When we went to Brighton on holiday my parents took me to see the *Pirates of Penzance* by Gilbert and Sullivan. I loved it! It was wonderful music for a child to hear! Daddy also drove us to London and to Southampton to see performances by the Bolshoi Ballet from Moscow.'

'Did your father play an instrument?' I asked Rachel. 'Yes, he played the piano, but he didn't read music. He could play music similar to Scott Joplin's by ear.' Joplin was dubbed 'The King of Ragtime.'

'Did your mother play?'

'No. She had her pony at the age of three and being outdoors was all she was interested in.'

On Saturdays from the age of eleven, said Rachel, she had violin lessons at the Dorset Rural Music School, a small house in Blandford's White Cliff Mill Street. The school was affiliated to the Royal College of Music. Joan would walk all the way from Number 8 Forum View, carrying Rachel's violin, and meet her after school at the music school, when she would sit with her through the lessons.

At the age of thirteen she started piano lessons too. 'All music lessons were private,' said Rachel, 'even though my parents could not really afford them.' In about 1960, the music school relocated to a house on the corner of Dorset Street and The Close.

Rachel's teachers informed her parents that they would like her to play in the National Youth Orchestra. 'I didn't have a clue about anything,' she said. 'I wasn't even curious. I just went and did it. I didn't think, "This is quite special."' For the occasion, Rachel was driven to London by her teacher, Miss Nancy Williams (a viola player), in her Morris Minor motor car, and they were accompanied by another violin teacher, Miss McGill. 'There was no problem about parking in London in those days!,' said Rachel. She then showed me a black and white photo of the National Youth Orchestra playing in the Royal Albert Hall, conducted by Sir Adrian Boult. 'That's me, second violin,' she said. 'Up until then I had always been first violin.' Of Sir Adrian, she said, 'Everybody loved him. He was so kind and didn't get stroppy.'

Blandford Grammar School's pavilion: Rachel and Vicky in 1964, 'leaving for our next tennis match'.

Rachel (aged seventeen) on tennis court at Blandford Grammar School, Bryanston church in background across the River Stour.

A music rehearsal in the Corn Exchange, Dorchester 1959, prior to performing in a concert in London. Rachel (aged fourteen): 'Me – 1st violins – 2nd row, 4th in! (immediately in front of conductor).

In 1959, when Rachel was aged fourteen, she and her parents joined the Aldermaston March. In February the previous year, the Campaign for Nuclear Disarmament (CND) was founded and at Easter some 5000 people marched in protest from London to Aldermaston, Berkshire, location of the Atomic Weapons Research Establishment (original project named 'High Explosive Research', renamed in 1952). Meanwhile the Communist Party, of which Arthur was a member, supported the peace movement and helped to develop the CND into a mass movement. The following year, and from then on, the route was reversed, from Aldermaston to Hyde Park in London, a distance of 52 miles. Marches were held over the Easter weekend.

Prior to the march, the Jordan family put surgical spirit on their feet for a fortnight in order to harden them up. 'There were no trainers in those days, of course,' said Rachel. 'On our way, we slept in school halls.' And on their arrival at Hyde Park, the marchers were addressed by Labour MP and political activist Tony Benn. The following year, when Rachel again joined the march with a boyfriend, it was philosopher and mathematician, Bertrand Russell who addressed the marchers.

Did Rachel believe in the CND and nuclear disarmament? The answer was an unequivocal 'Yes. Young people didn't want any bombs.' 'And now?' 'I suppose we just have to live with them,' she replied with a frown.

In 1959, Rachel's mother, Joan took a job at Poole Pottery for a couple of months. 'That was in order to fund my trip with the school to the

Rachel (aged sixteen) in 1961: 'The photo, taken by my boyfriend, won the local Amateur Photography Society's 1st prize'.

Rachel (aged sixteen) with 'Jipp' at 8 Forum View, Bryanston in 1961: 'My little dog from 1958. She lived to be thirteen'.

Blandford Grammar School Orchestra, 1961. Rachel: 'I am first on the left in paisley silk dress (hair up), aged sixteen'.

1960 Summer Olympic Games in Rome. For Mummy, it meant walking down The Drive to catch the Hants & Dorset service bus which would take her the 12 miles to Poole; then walking down the High Street to Poole Quay and the pottery.' What did Rachel think of the Olympics? 'We watched a football match. That was pretty boring! Then we saw Ian Black in the swimming pool competing in the 400 metres freestyle. But we were 100 feet or so up in the air, and the competitors looked like little pins! But we did see the sights of Rome. That was the best part of it!'

Rachel with 'Jipp' and the famous Ford Consul.

The following year, Joan took a job at Blandford Cottage Hospital, where she worked for three years, walking the 2 miles plus there, and 2 miles plus back, every day.

In summer 1962, when she was seventeen, Rachel and her grammar school friend, Diane were chosen to be extras in the film 'Tom Jones', starring Albert Finney and released on 27 June 1963. Her scene was filmed at Sutton Poyntz near Weymouth, commencing at 5 a.m.!

16

The Jordan Family's Visits to Eastern Europe

The Soviet Union (USSR) was created from the Russian Empire in the aftermath of the 1917 Russian Revolution. It comprised 12 republics, one of which was Russia. Between 1938 and 1945, the following states were annexed by the Soviet Union: Estonia, Lithuania, Latvia, Byelorussia, Ukraine, Moldavia (Moldova); and the following countries became satellites of the Soviet Union: East Germany (officially the German Democratic Republic), Czechoslovakia, Hungary, Poland, Yugoslavia, Romania, Bulgaria, Albania, Austria (Soviet zone).

By virtue of his position as Dorset Area Organizer for the National Union of Agricultural Workers, Arthur had forged links with similar trade unions in East Germany, Czechoslovakia, and Hungary, to which countries he and his family were invited. 'We were given the "red carpet" treatment,' said Rachel.

'In 1952, when I was aged seven, Mummy visited Czechoslovakia with six boys and six girls on an exchange visit. She brought me back a doll dressed in national costume.' So, Rachel did have a doll to play with? 'No, not one to play with. This was an ornate, decorative doll. It was only for display. In fact, at every Eastern European country we subsequently visited, I would be given a beautiful doll, hand-made and in traditional national costume. I soon built up

Rachel (aged thirteen) and Arthur on a visit to Thüringia, East Germany in 1958.

quite a collection and always bought a doll in its national costume from every country in Europe which we visited on our camping holidays.'

'In 1955, when I was aged ten, we visited East Germany. On our arrival, we were driven in two chauffeur driven cars: my father in one, and Mummy and me in the other. At every town we stopped at for lunch, we found that the restaurant had been forewarned, and long tables had been laid out and draped with the East German and UK flags. At one meal, they served up a freshwater fish, beautifully decorated. This was food that no ordinary East German could afford. But the food, I hated it. All I wanted was egg and chips! So, they brought me what they called a "farmer's breakfast" – omelette with pieces of ham in it! I sat at the far end of the table with the two chauffeurs for hours, through five or six courses, whilst earnest conversations took place. This was with the aid of interpreters, though Daddy did speak some German. We were given a tour of big state cooperative farms, shown how the machinery worked, and treated to more banquets.'

'The following year, we were invited back to East Germany, this time for a relaxing holiday in a luxury holiday home in Thüringia, with its beautiful forests. We drove there and found that the people were in awe of us. They had never seen anybody from the West, and they said, "Mustn't it be wonderful in the West where they have such lovely cars!"'

'Every East German worker, no matter what their sphere of work was, could take two weeks holiday per year with their family at minimal cost. Every morning before breakfast the manager, attired in lederhosen, would stand outside in the forecourt and blow a whistle. Whereupon all the guests appeared on the balcony to do exercises. I didn't!'

'In East Germany every university student was required to do an ordinary job for four weeks of the summer recess. Our waitress's name was Adelheid and she was a medical student. One day she asked my parents if she could take me to visit her home. Her father was a jeweller, and I was invited to choose a piece of jewellery. I chose a solid silver bangle, which I always wore.'

'We were taken to the Meissen factory, near Dresden, where Mummy and Daddy were presented with two beautiful pieces of Meissen. I was given a lovely little oblong trinket box. The East Germans also gave my parents a pair of opera glasses and Daddy, a Leica camera, which was top of the range in those days. We were also taken to see a glass blowing factory, where I chose a row of elephants of decreasing size. I loved them and I've kept them with me all my life: in my bedroom as a child, and in various bathrooms in places where we lived.'

'In Potsdam, we were shown into a great big room where the eponymous Potsdam Agreement was signed on 1 August 1945, and the great big armchairs in which Soviet Union Secretary General, Josef Stalin; US President, Harry S. Truman; and UK Prime Minister, Clement Atlee, who were the signatories, had sat.' This was the agreement concerning the post-war military occupation of Germany and the reconstitution of its borders.

'One of my favourite dolls,' said Rachel, 'was one which I chose in East Germany as a gift from the trade union officials, I called him "The Little Old Man". His coat, stockings, boots were all hand stitched, and his face was hand painted.'

Rachel doing a 'Super Fiendish Sudoku', watched by 'The Little Old Man', a gift to her from trade union officials in East Germany.

'On our return to England, I wore the bangle that Adelheid had given me to school. There was an argument with my teachers because pupils were not permitted to wear jewellery. Daddy then asked the headmaster, "why then are some children wearing crucifixes?" The outcome was that I was suspended for three days, and we had to give in, but we had made our point.'

'When Daddy visited Czechoslovakia, he brought me back two hand-made, wooden marionettes with clothes made of felt. He made a stage, and with these marionettes, held a puppet show for the children of our village, who numbered about ten in all.'

A visit by the Jordan family to Hungary in 1962, when Rachel was aged seventeen, was to have unforeseen consequences. 'We were invited to Hungary by the Hungarian Trade Union Movement, and we decided to combine it with a holiday, so we camped at Lake Balaton. In Budapest, I bought a Hungarian doll, from the only souvenir shop. The shop was state run, and everything for sale was hand-made by peasants in the countryside.'

'We camped at Lake Balaton and took our evening meals at a nearby hotel, and this is where I met Gabor, a student of engineering, who would be my future husband.'

17

Arthur is Frustrated in his Hopes for Rachel

It was Arthur's dream that Rachel should embrace the same Marxist views as he did. What did her mother, Joan have to say about that? 'Mummy just went along with it, as she always did with everything,' said Rachel.

'It was also Daddy's dearest wish that I should become a doctor. He lived his life vicariously through me and he was desperate for me to achieve what he had not had the opportunity to do. Daddy gave me books on how to become a doctor and on the history of medicine when I was only thirteen! I wanted to train as a nurse!'

'At the grammar school, at a meeting to which the parents were invited, but not the children, my form teacher told my father that I was better suited to the arts than the sciences. But Daddy overruled him.' What subjects would Rachel have chosen, given the choice? 'French, and History. Biology was all right, I suppose. But I hated English!' In the event, she took Physics, Chemistry, and Biology for 'A' level.

'I was granted an interview at the University of Bristol's medical school and on the way in the car, Daddy said, 'They're going to ask you why you want to become a doctor'. 'But I don't want to be a doctor.' But he carried on regardless. 'You want to be a doctor because you want to help people and make a better world.' 'But I want to be a nurse and make a better world.' But Rachel need not have worried. She was turned down on the grounds that 'women, once qualified, simply leave to have babies and we never see them again.'

'I passed my A-levels in chemistry and biology, but failed physics, despite having had private tuition. Daddy then urged me to become a teacher. Finally, he threw in the towel and at the age of nineteen, I commenced at St Mary's Hospital, Paddington, as a student nurse. One needed "A" Levels to get into any of London's four teaching hospitals. I was accepted by all four but chose St Mary's on account of Dr Alexander Fleming's work there when he discovered penicillin.'

'Why were you so intent on becoming a nurse, rather than a doctor as your father wished,' I asked Rachel.

PTS nurses at St Mary's Hospital, Paddington, 1964. Rachel (top left).

'When I was aged twelve or thirteen, I read a book called *Sue Barton: Student Nurse*, and I thought it sounded rather good.' First published in 1936, it was by US author Helen Dore Boylston.

'I didn't want to be a doctor. It didn't appeal to me. And then a program called "Emergency Ward 10" was broadcast on the television, at 7:30 every Tuesday and Friday evenings. We had no television, so I went next door to watch it. I loved it. I still remember Dr Latimer, who was the really handsome doctor in it.'

"Emergency Ward 10" was a British medical soap opera shown on ITV between 1957 and 1967. The first episode was shown on 19 February 1957. 'Dr Latimer' was played by John Carson. He fell in love with 'Nurse Carole Young', played by Jill Browne.

'But I never think doctors have much to do with their patients. They come and go, and they say a bit, but they keep their distance. They leave nurses to do the job of giving bad news, at least, that was how it used to be. Nowadays, perhaps they are more empathetic, and empathy is part of their training. There was nothing like that when I trained. Also, I liked the thought of the uniform. At that age, you're quite impressionable.'

At first, Rachel's words came as a shock to me. But then I realised that what had initially made me want to become a doctor was a desire to learn about the various diseases to which the human body is susceptible, and of the great medical breakthroughs that have been made in the past. Penicillin, for example, was discovered by Dr Alexander Fleming at St Mary's Hospital Paddington, which is where Rachel underwent her nursing training, and the drug was subsequently first tested at my alma mater, Oxford's Radcliffe Infirmary.

18

Arthur Sticks his Neck Out

The July-December 1962 issue of *Land and Labour* (published by the Trade Union International of Agricultural, Forestry, and Plantation Workers) was 'dedicated to the Preparations of the IVth World Conference of Agricultural, Forestry, and Plantation Workers' Trade Unions', to be held from the 20th to the 24th of November of that year in the Bulgarian capital, Sofia. Among the contributors to the issue was Arthur, whose article was entitled 'Britain: Problems of Farm Workers'.

Arthur began by stating that 'The main features of British agriculture since the Second World War have been the large increase in production, the high level of mechanisation, and the drastic reduction in the number of workers employed on the farms. Unfortunately, the farm workers had not improved their position in the same proportion as the increased productivity for their employers.'

'The standard of living of farm workers has not kept pace with these developments; neither has it kept pace with the improvements gained by most industrial workers during the post-war period.' As a result of this increased mechanisation, tractors and combine harvesters had virtually replaced the working horses. Arthur produced detailed statistics to back up his points.

'In order to understand farm workers in the struggle for better wages and working conditions it has to be understood that the whole agricultural industry, both farmers and farm workers are confronted by monopoly capitalism.' This is defined as a capitalist system typified by trade monopolies in the hands of a few people.

In the UK, said Arthur, 'the majority of the farmers are on small acreages, and many are not making a much better living than the farm workers. This means that they are unable to stand up to the big monopoly firms which sell to agriculture, and which buy the produce from it.'

Arthur believed that there was 'scope for increasing both efficiency and total production, in the course of which the living standard of the farmers and the farmworkers could be tremendously improved. However, such a way forward is impossible until monopoly capitalism is defeated, and a government elected to carry out a socialist policy laying the basis for a Socialist Britain.'

Arthur quoted from a Meeting of the 81 Communist Parties in Moscow in 1960, where it was affirmed that state monopoly capitalism 'closely combines the power of the monopolies with that of the state with the aim of saving the capitalist system and increasing the profits of the imperialist bourgeoisie [middle class] to the upmost by exploiting the working-class and plundering large sections of the population.'

Arthur referred to the Agricultural Wages Board, which was set up under an Act of Parliament. Although it included representatives of both the NUAW and of the National Farmers Union, it was the chairman and four members, described as 'independent', 'upon whom the decision usually rests, and these independent members are also influenced by the government's attitude to wages when the negotiations are in progress.'

Arthur now addressed the vexed question of land nationalisation. 'It is part of the policy of the National Union of Agricultural Workers to call for the public ownership of the land, and it is suggested that a start should be made by the Government taking over the large, landed estates in which the farmers are tenants. Such a step might bring into public ownership about 60% of the total acreage and the same percentage of farms.'

'The Communist Party of Great Britain, in its own program for agriculture "Farming to Feed Britain" also advocated the development of a number of State farms to serve as experimental farms and to demonstrate to the private farmers the advantages of large-scale methods and modern techniques.'

Finally, Arthur turned his attention to the 'Common Market' (European Economic Community). If the United Kingdom was to join that organisation, he feared that 'a change in the price structure of Britain's agriculture will be demanded by the other member countries. Under pressure from the government, pressure from "Brussels", and pressure from monopoly capitalism at home, the farmers will inevitably seek to solve their problems at the expense of the farm workers. That is why the workers are expressing strong opposition to Britain joining the Common Market.' The NUAW was fully aware that the 1962 World Conference was taking place and had decided against sending a representative to it.

When he composed his article, Arthur could have been in no doubt that it would come to the union's attention. In fact, the NUAW reacted in the following way, stating that:

'In an article appearing in a journal of this kind the Union could not take any exception to it excepting on two points, both of which occur on page 43. The first implies the Union is expressing strong opposition to Britain joining the Common Market. The second mis-states NUAW policy on nationalisation to make it sound as if it agrees with the Communist Party policy on the same subject.'

'However, since the article is signed by Arthur Jordan, and it is specifically stated that he is the District Organizer for the Dorset branch of a the NUAW, the article is open to criticism on a number of other points, all of which are marked. Clearly, the article will be taken by those who read it as representing the considered views of the NUAW, and many of the things that are said would never be agreed on if this statement was submitted either to the EC [Executive Committee of the NUAW] or to the Biennial Conference before publication.'

Had the article been unsigned, or written under a pen-name, 'in that case we could have no cause for complaint except where mis-statements of fact occur'.

There is no question that Arthur was honest and sincere in his beliefs. But why did he not give the NUAW a sight of that article before he sent it to *Land and Labour*? Presumably because he knew the union would amend it.

The points made by the union appear to be fair and valid. Arthur, as a union member, had been guilty of misrepresentation in front of an international audience of readers. Furthermore, his reference to the Communist Party would be taken as provocative. What, if any, would the repercussions be? Arthur was soon to find out.

19
Arthur is Dismissed from his Post
Protests

News of NUAW's activities in the various counties of England was published in the *Landworker*, the monthly journal of the NUAW. In the issue of January 1963, in an entry which ran to almost half a page, it was reported that 'Bro. Jordan (Organizer) spoke on the future for farm workers'. In respect of the threatened closure of Blandford's local railway line, 'Bro. Jordan was able to make a statement putting the agricultural workers' point of view and indicating the hardship that would be caused for rural people if the line was closed'; 'A Sunday School at Sherborne, organized by the WEA [Workers Educational Association, a voluntary sector provider of adult education founded in 1903] had Bro. Jordan as chairman and the subject was "Agriculture and the Common Market".'

'About half the attendance of thirty were union members.' It was also reported that 'Bro. Jordan attended meetings of forestry workers in the Hole Common, Chideock, and Beaminster areas.' Finally, 'Bro. E. [Ernie] Amey (NUAW Secretary, Farnham, Dorset) organized a successful meeting at Ashmore, when Bro. Jordan spoke on the future for farm workers.'

This testifies to Arthur's industriousness and dedication. However, by the time the above article was published in the *Landworker*, he had already been dismissed as Dorset Organizer for the NUAW.

As a trade union organizer, who was also a Communist, Arthur had arrived in rural Dorset in 1945 and preached first Socialism, and shortly afterwards, Communism. However, the odds of him being successful were slim, for several reasons. For example, the North Dorset parliamentary constituency, of which Blandford was a part, was created in 1885, and since then, not a single elected MP had been from the Labour Party. There had been nine Conservatives, four Liberals, and two Unionists. As for Communism, there was little or no appetite for it either among the NUAW hierarchy or among the farm workers themselves, as Arthur discovered. The aristocracy and gentry saw it as a dangerous and destabilising influence, and the farmers did not exactly welcome someone who was constantly pressing for an increase in the workers' wages. As for the agricultural worker members of the NUAW, they were prepared to turn a blind eye to Arthur's political beliefs, because they recognised that he was doing his utmost to assist them. But now, it seems, he had gone too far.

'I was with Daddy when he attended his hearing at Number 308, Gray's Inn Road, the London headquarters of the NUAW,' said Rachel. That was on 21 December 1962, only four days before Christmas

'He came out and told me the bad news; that he had been sacked on the spot from his position as Dorset Organizer of the NUAW by its Executive Committee. We found a phone box and he telephoned Mummy with the news. Then he said, "Let's go to a restaurant and eat!" It was a Greek Cypriot restaurant.'

On the same day, Harold Collison, General Secretary of the NUAW, wrote to Arthur as follows:

'Dear Bro. Jordan,

This is to confirm the decision of the Executive Committee taken at their meeting today, conveyed to you by the vice president Bro. Hilton on their behalf, that having very carefully considered certain aspects of your recent and past activities they came to the conclusion that they had no alternative than to dismiss you as from this date.'

The Press reported Collison as saying that Arthur had dismissed 'for actions where he had not conformed to Union Policy', although he did add that, 'Mr Jordan was a good organizer'.

What were the reasons given for Arthur's sacking? In a statement to the press, which was published in the *Country Standard* winter edition of 1963, Arthur stated that the NAUW's Executive Committee had objected to his:

1. Writing an article in the Dorset NUAW Bulletin demanding higher pay for farm workers and contrasting their pay with that of the police and mentioning the latter's [presumably heavy handed] method of dealing with ban-the-bomb demonstrators.

2. Accepting an invitation to speak to Salisbury Trades Council before obtaining the permission of the General Secretary, although no date has been fixed and it was made clear to the TC [Trades Council] secretary on the phone that he should have to have Head Office permission.

3. Writing an article (albeit in a strictly personal capacity) about British agriculture in *Land and Labour*, a journal of the World Federation of Trade Unions.

4. Reporting in the Dorset Bulletin and in the *Land and Labour* article that a majority of both farm workers and farmers are expressing opposition to the Common Market.

5. Reporting (correctly) in the article large numbers of resolutions

calling for a more determined attitude by the Executive Committee to secure a £10 wage for farm workers.

6. Inviting a member of the union from another district to participate in a television programme. On this issue, the EC accepted his explanation.

'This was not the first time that the EC had interviewed Jordan about similar matters, but he categorically denied the General Secretary's statement reported in the Press to the effect that he had not conformed to union policy. He remained understandably bitter about this episode for the rest of his life, but often reflected upon the compensation he had secured on behalf of his members' i.e. as NUAW Organizer.

Rachel believed that her father would never have been dismissed had Edwin Gooch, President of the NUAW from 1928 (until his death in 1964) had his way. 'President Gooch was a good man,' said Rachel, 'and Daddy liked him. Daddy would meet him off the train at Dorchester Station when he came down from London. He would never have got rid of Daddy. Harold Collison, who became General Secretary of the NUAW in 1953, however, always had it in for Daddy, but he had to wait several years before he managed to get rid of him. There was no love lost between Collison and Daddy.'

Joan Maynard was disgusted. Professor and educationalist Kristine Mason O'Connor said of Joan that she 'had admired Arthur Jordan and felt the Executive Committee [of the NUAW] had been trying for years to be rid of him, fearing he would be elected General Secretary when the vacancy arose.' And Kristine quoted Joan as saying, 'They really were a load of bastards. I never forgot that. What they were doing was against the interests of the members, that's what I couldn't stand; this man was crushed, a wonderful representative of the members. They chopped off our head when they chopped off Arthur; he was a great inspiration to us all.'

Joan Maynard. Photo: People's History Museum, Left Bank, Spinningfields, Manchester.

Joan Maynard, said Kristine, 'tried to persuade Arthur Jordan to demand a recall of the Biennial Conference to overturn the Executive Committee's decision – membership of the Communist Party was not a breach of Union rules.' However, Arthur 'was unwilling, fearing the publicity would prevent him ever getting another job.'

The outcome was, said Rachel, 'that we left Dorset, and Daddy left behind those loyal people' i.e. the Dorset NUAW members 'and they never heard from him again.'

Nonetheless, despite all, on 28 January 1963 General Secretary Collison wrote to Arthur enclosing a generous reference:

'To Whom it may Concern'

'Mr Arthur Jordan of 8 Forum View, Bryanston, Blandford Forum, Dorset was employed by us as a district officer for sixteen years. During that time, he put his fullest energies into his work, a large part of which depended on working on his own initiative. His employment involved him in financial transactions and in this respect his behaviour was impeccable. His attention to detail showed him to have above average organising ability we are quite sure that Mr Jordan will always give of his best in any work which he is convinced is worthwhile.'

In terms of results achieved, there is no doubt that Arthur was outstanding. For example, before the Second World War, Dorset had 74 NUAW branches. When he commenced as Organizer for Dorset in 1946, there were 91 branches. And by 1958 that figure had risen to 105 branches. This was despite the fact the NUAM membership nationally had passed its peak of 137,000 in 1948.

There were immediate protests at Arthur's dismissal, an indication of the high regard and esteem in which he was held, and the interest from the Press was intense. 'There were TV reporters and cameras outside our home,' said Rachel, 'so we drew the curtains and laid low.'

According to the minutes of the Dorset County Committee 'a resolution calling for Jordan's reinstatement' was 'passed, unanimously', and furthermore, the committee 'sent a deputation to the EC [Executive Committee] to argue its case.' And the minutes of the Wimborne District NUAW Committee dated 25 January 1963, under the heading 'Dismissal of Organizer', stated that 'A deputation appointed by the County [NUAW] Committee to wait upon the [NUAW] Executive Committee had been to London on the 24th January and had argued very strongly that the EC should reinstate Bro. Jordan.'

'Jess Waterman offered to organize a protest on Daddy's behalf,' said Rachel, 'but Daddy said no because once again, he feared it might jeopardise his chances of ever getting another job.'

The protests were to no avail. The decision stood, and on 19 April 1963, Bro. Frederick Cole, the Sherborne District NUAW Committee Chairman, was appointed NUAW Organizer for Dorset in Arthur's place.

There were many tributes to Arthur, who since his arrival in Dorset, had doubled the NUAW's membership in that county.

20

Aftermath

In January 1962, Arthur and Joan moved to London, said Rachel, 'where that summer Daddy was offered a job with the British Airline Pilots Association. However, a month later he was sacked by them too, once they found out that he was a member of the Communist Party. I spent six weeks of that summer in Hungary with Gabor, to whom I was now engaged to be married. When I returned from Hungary, my parents met me at Victoria Station and took me to our new home: a large modern flat which they were renting in Woking. I did not return to Bryanston; I did not see my friends again; I did not even have their postal addresses.'

'When Mummy received an inheritance from a great aunt of £3000, she and Arthur purchased a large Victorian house, Number 98, Venner Road, Sydenham, in Kent. Meanwhile, I commenced at a teacher training college in Exeter but returned home within a fortnight as I hated every minute of it! I had never wanted to become a teacher, but Daddy insisted.'

Arthur now found employment with Collets Bookshop, based in Charing Cross Road, London. The firm was founded in 1934 by the wealthy Eva Collet Reckitt, a longstanding member of the Communist Party. Collets imported communist and radical publications.

In 1964, whilst at Collets, Arthur met Elisabeth Frood, the daughter of a Liverpool teacher. Elisabeth, who was the niece of Dodi, a friend of the Jordan family from Camden Town, was the firm's canteen manageress. In that year, Arthur was tasked with organising the relocation of the Collets' Company from London to Wellingborough, Northamptonshire, under the London Overspill Scheme. It was government policy to relocate residents from Greater London to other parts of the country. At Wellingborough, the staff at Collets, many of whom were Communist Party members, were active in the Union of Shop, Distributive and Allied Workers and dominated the local Communist Party branch.

Meanwhile, Joan went to stay, temporarily, with her brother, David on his farm in Herefordshire; Arthur went to stay with Dodi.

'In spring 1964, at the age of eighteen,' said Rachel, 'I enrolled as a student nurse at St Mary's Hospital Paddington. When I was there, I had a telephone call. The London office of the magazine *Harper's Bazaar* asked me to do a few "shoots". At the grammar school my boyfriend Nigel, who was a keen amateur photographer, had sent the magazine a photo of me and this was their response.' Was her photo published in the magazine? 'I never looked, to be honest. I didn't rush about to see if I was in *Harpers*. I just wanted the money!'

'However, I left St Mary's in spring 1965 after only one year, as you had to give up nursing if you got married, as I was intending to do. I now went to live with Mummy in Sydenham. Meanwhile, Joan had obtained work as an animal technician at the Medical Research Council [MRC] in Carshalton.'

'My fiancé, Gabor came over from Hungary for six weeks in the summer of 1965 during his university vacation, and he asked Daddy for permission to marry me. I was only twenty at the time. Gabor was at Budapest University, on a four-year course studying electronic engineering. Whereupon, Daddy told me, 'That's it then! You will never do anything with your life!' Arthur believed, mistakenly, that in the Eastern Bloc countries it was the norm for married women to stay at home, as in the UK.

On Friday 1 October 1965, Arthur wrote to Joan from 17 Shakespeare Road, Wellingborough, Northants. 'Daddy told Mummy that he would not be returning to the family home,' said Rachel, 'and that he intended to start a new life with Elisabeth Frood.' Arthur admitted that 'such a decision' by him 'could not have been made at a more difficult time' for both Joan and Rachel. Nevertheless, he said, 'I feel that, by and large, I have always done the best thing for Rachel. I know that for years I organized my time very largely to be with her. Those were wonderfully happy days, but now she is a self-reliant person, and I can do no more for now. However, always I will be happy to meet her or help her if she wishes it and if I can do so.'

Finally, to Joan, he wrote, 'Nothing I have said, or will say, in any way implies that there is or ever has been a single fault on your side. I believe you to be a fine person, and to have been a splendid partner during our married life.'

The Sydenham house was sold, and a local estate agent, who was sympathetic to the Communist cause, now found Joan a first-floor flat in a Victorian house which was due for demolition. 'We moved into it with my little dog, Jipp,' said Rachel. This meant that when the house was demolished, Jean would automatically be offered a new council flat. 'This was on the 6th floor with wonderful views of Crystal Palace Park and its woods, and she was delighted.' Joan would now make new friends at her MRC workplace, including Ken Livingstone, the Council's Chief Animal Technician. Livingstone would later became Mayor of London and a labour M.P. Also, unlike Arthur, Joan kept in touch with her Dorset friends, including Ellen and Johnny Dunford, who had relocated from Forum View, Bryanston, to a bungalow at 19 Philip Road, Blandford. And in her holidays, Joan stayed with Gladys ('Glad') Shears in Winterborne Kingston. Glad's husband was Les, Secretary of the Winterborne Kingston branch of the NUAW. She also kept in close touch with Helen Dunman in Swanage.

On 20 December 1965, Rachel applied for a job at the headquarters of the administration department of the London Ambulance Service near County Hall, Waterloo, SE 1. 'I seemed to get every job I applied for,' she said, but 'I honestly didn't have a clue what I was doing, and I never did have! They took me just because I had "A" levels. At lunchtime I crossed Westminster Bridge and was in the City of London.'

Despite her modesty, Rachel must have been well thought of because when she resigned on 13 May 1966, the staff had a collection for her, and with the money, she purchased some towels, from 'a posh shop' in Regent Street!

In June 1966, Rachel departed for Hungary, leaving her dog, Jipp in the care of her mother.

21

For Rachel, Hungary Beckons
Marriage: Life Behind the 'Iron Curtain'

In June 1966, Rachel departed for Hungary and its capital, Budapest, which in those days was behind the 'Iron Curtain' – a metaphor for a political, military, and ideological barrier erected by the Soviet Union at the end of the Second World War, separating the Soviet bloc and the West – to live with Gabor and his parents. She left Jipp in the care of her mother.

Prior to Rachel leaving for Hungary, Arthur wrote to her as follows, with reference to their recent meeting:

'I was of course so happy to receive both your letters and especially the first which told me that you had enjoyed our evening together. I did, so very much, Rachel, and I just wish we could do it more often now that the time is drawing near when you will leave this country. I realise how precious to me are the brief hours we shall be able to spend together. Perhaps we can fix another meeting.'

Arthur revealed to Rachel the deep remorse he felt at breaking up the family, especially at this important time in her life:

'As you probably know, I have not known 'cheerfulness' myself for a long time now. This has been partly the result of events and their impact on me and partly my own state of mind. It is all such a contradiction – my philosophy and my own peace of mind. I had reached the very depths of despair some months ago. Today, I am not so depressed as then but even so I cannot find real peace of mind. Frankly, Rachel, the happiness

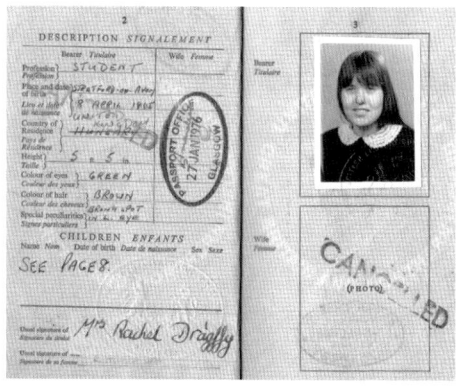

Rachel's passport, issued to her when she was sixteen, which she used for her journeys to Hungary.

which Elisabeth brings me in numerous ways is offset by my unhappy feeling when I reflect upon my having broken up a family unit and caused problems and unhappiness for other people. Above all, I am depressed that I should have taken this step in what is going to be such an important year in your life – you'll be twenty-one and you'll get married, and you'll leave this country. The number of times we'll meet in years to come will be few.'

'However, the important thing is what is new, arising and developing and it's you and your married life that is new. I wish you such joy and happiness – both of you. I am a little disappointed that I won't be at your wedding for we've been together in so many events – good and not so good.'

Here, Arthur was surely remembering their holidays, games of tennis together, the birthday parties that he and Joan had organized for Rachel and her friends and taking his daughter with him in his car on his visits to NUAW members throughout the county.

'My thoughts and sincerest wishes will be for you on that day.'

Arthur now paid tribute to Joan:

'Whilst writing on this theme Rachel, I want to say this. Most people who know you say complimentary things to me about you. Some compliment me on having such a daughter. I know and recognise and will forever acknowledge that to the extent parents contributed to what you are, then Mummy is to be congratulated perhaps more than myself.'

Arthur now reaffirmed his belief in Marxism which, he said:

'...taught me all that I know that is good, so the extent I have done any good deeds, it has been a result of my Marxist learning.'

'I have never really found my feet since I was sacked from the NUAW. Twenty years in that job with its opportunities to serve the cause I believe in made a deeper impression on me than I realised at the time. However, my convictions are unshaken Rachel, and I shall find my way back to more political work than of late. As a start, I may do a [Communist] Party class for new members here soon.'

Arthur ended by describing Joan as 'a fine comrade and mother. I truly wish her happiness and hope she is well.

My deep love to you Rachel, Daddy.'

What were Rachel's feelings about her mother being left alone when she went to live in Hungary? 'I was young,' she said, with tears in her eyes. 'I had no idea about the implication of things. I wasn't really bothered about where I went, or what I did. I just went with the flow. Women followed their husbands in those days, and they went where the work was.'

'I took the train across Europe to Hungary,' said Rachel. 'Most English people didn't know where Hungary lay on the map. Everyone thought

I was really brave. There were border guards with guns, but I wasn't scared of anything. I didn't know what the fuss was about!'

On Sunday 17 July 1966, Rachel and Gabor were married in the Hungarian capital, Budapest, in the central registry office, next to the Parliament buildings. Joan attended the wedding with Dodi, travelling there by train. 'Thereafter, Mummy made several visits to us in Hungary, on one of which she broke her ankle whilst riding a horse!'

Rachel and Gabor arrived for their honeymoon at a hotel on the Danube Bend, where 'everyone was watching the football World Cup on the hotel's one TV. Nobody could believe that there were any English people – i.e. me – there!' On 30 July, England won the final by defeating Germany 4-2.

Rachel and Gabor on their wedding day.

The couple lived with Gabor's parents in Budapest (in what once was an aristocratic home) and they made Rachel thoroughly welcome. The house had large rooms with high ceilings, big double doors, and a terraced veranda. Her father-in-law, Gyula, married to Edit, was from an aristocratic background, as the 'ffy' in his surname, 'Drágffy' signified.

'Gyula had purchased a plot of land at Lake Balaton, and at about the time I arrived in Hungary, the building of a villa had commenced on the site. So, we spent every summer holiday down at the lake.'

Rachel enjoyed learning about Hungarian cuisine. In those days everything was prepared from scratch (apart from bread). There were no such thing as frozen foods. There were no refrigerators until about 1968.

Rachel enrolled at a special language school which was for the children of foreign diplomats. Commencing in August 1966, she now spent six hours a day learning Hungarian.

Did Rachel and Gabor ever discuss politics? 'Why would I want to? I'm a woman, for God's sake! I had more important things to do!'

In December 1966, Gabor applied for and was offered a job in Hampshire, UK with an electronics firm. 'There was no problem in us leaving the country,' said Rachel. But next time they left Hungary circumstances would be entirely different! 'We rented a caravan in Aldershot,' said Rachel, 'in order to save money, and Gabor bought a second-hand Renault Dauphine, which was so old it had to be patched up with fibreglass! Meanwhile, I got a job as a secretary.'

In summer 1967, Rachel and Gabor were visited by Arthur. 'Daddy came down from Northamptonshire, bringing an apple pie that Elisabeth had made, and we had a picnic at Littlehampton, West Sussex.' She would not see her father again for thirty-seven long years!

Rachel's certificate from the Hungarian language school.

In June 1967, Rachel returned alone by train to Hungary where she stayed with her in-laws, prior to taking the language examination. She was then joined by Gabor and Joan. 'Mummy drove Gabor in the Renault Dauphine as he had no driving licence.' Why was that? 'Because in Hungary he had not possessed a car. Nobody in Hungary had a car.'

'Mummy stayed on with us in Budapest for a three-week holiday. In autumn 1967, I enrolled at the University of Budapest to study foreign languages and international trade, but having become fluent in Hungarian, I chose English and French as my two foreign languages! Lectures in Hungarian were not easy for me, and I found myself sobbing because to begin with, I found it impossible to listen to the lecturer and take notes at the same time. But my Hungarian fellow students helped me out.'

'Prior to and during the Second World War, the second language for Hungarians was German. Hungary was "liberated" by the Soviets in 1945, and it became a Communist state in 1949. From then on, the youth of Hungary was required to learn Russian as a second language. But when I was there in the 1960s, Hungarians were encouraged to learn English. After all, if you only spoke Hungarian, nobody else would understand you!'

'One day, I was invited by a Hungarian Radio Station to join four or five other UK citizens – who were from the British Embassy. We were to read plays aloud, each of us taking the part of a character, for a recording. I was told that this was so Hungarians could get used to hearing English.'

'I was short of money at the time, as I only had my monthly payment from the government to help out with university expenses, and Gabor likewise. I should point out that the grades you were awarded in your exams determined how much the payments were, so everyone struggled to achieve top grades in order to receive maximum money. I therefore accepted the invitation and the radio station paid me well!'

In 1969, before Rachel had completed her degree course, she and Gabor made the decision to leave the country for good. They told nobody of their plans, not even his parents, before making their 'escape'.

Had Rachel enjoyed her time in Hungary? 'Yes, I loved it!,' she replied without hesitation. But this was not to say that she was unaware of the poverty, corruption and unfairness that existed in that country, although there was no such thing as unemployment!

Gabor and Rachel skating on the lake at Vidám Park, Budapest, in 1964. Agricultural Museum in background.

Rachel with canine companion in Hungarian mountains, winter 1964.

22
Rachel's Remarkable Hungarian In-Laws!

The Drágffy family, into which Rachel had married, was impacted by both the Nazi invasion of Hungary in 1944, and by subsequent 'liberation' of that country by the Soviet Union in 1945.

On 20 November 1940 Hungary had joined the Axis powers – Germany, Italy, and Japan – the Second World War having commenced on 1 September 1939. However, on 19 March 1944 the Nazis invaded Hungary, after its Prime Minister Miklós Kállay had engaged in peace negotiations with the US and the UK.

Miklós Drágffy (1905-1989). (Nicholas, or 'Uncle Miki'), Rachel's uncle-in-law

Nicholas studied law at Budapest; Dresden, Germany; Oxford, UK; and the Sorbonne, Paris. It was at the Sorbonnne that Nicholas met his wife-to-be Elisabeth ('Lily') van Peski (1902-1980) from Rotterdam, Holland. After their marriage in 1937, the couple set up home in Budapest, where Nicholas worked in the French Embassy. Two years later, he joined the Hungarian Ministry of Foreign Affairs.

Prior to the Nazi occupation of Hungary, 'it was said', that Nicholas:

'…was part of a secret Hungarian delegation to negotiate special armistice with the Western Allies. The German Gestapo was informed about the Hungarian intention and in March 1944, Germany promptly occupied Hungary.'

Nicholas and Lily now escaped to France, from where they travelled to New Caledonia (an archipelago in the south-west Pacific Ocean, then a French colony).

'Nicholas gave up his profession and while Lily worked in Sydney, Australia, he made his living from fishing. He mentioned in a number of his letters to the family back in Hungary that he was visited by Hungarians whom he suspected worked for the secret service. The fact that he had worked for the French Embassy and then for the Hungarian Ministry of

Foreign Affairs, and that he "escaped" to a French colony at the other end of the world, gives rise to speculation that he might have been recruited by the French Secret Service.'[1]

In the early 1960s, Nicholas and Lily relocated to Holland, the land of Lily's birth. They now set up home in a converted windmill, the 'Aeolus' in Dreischor, the Netherlands.

An article in the Netherlands newspaper *Zierikzeesche Nieuwsbode* dated 10 September 1982 stated as follows:

'The mill "Aeolus" in Dreischor has been inhabited for twenty years by Dr Nicholas Drágffy.' Eight years prior to the 'Drágffy couple' – i.e. Nicholas and Lily – occupying the mill, 'it had been completely restored'. 'The mill was then called "De Koekoek". Merrour (Madam – i.e. Lily) Drágffy later discovered that "Aeolus" or "God of the Winds" was one of the [its] original names. She then hastened to rename the mill.' This was because she did not like the name 'De Koekoek'.

'The mill "Aeolus" was built in 1739 by order of the craftsman [presumably architect] Mr Jan Daniel Ockerse.' This was a flour mill, which 'was in operation until 1962: grain was ground for cattle feed, but also for human consumption'. In other words, this had been a working mill, which was converted into living accommodation prior to the arrival of the Drágffys.[2] As an extension to the mill, Nicholas added a library and a dressing room.

The 'Aeolus', Dreischor, Holland, late 1960s.

In the late 1960s Rachel and Gábor paid Nicholas and Lily a visit and they stayed at the mill. For Nicholas, the tragedy was that because of the existence of the 'Iron Curtain', he was prevented from contacting his other relatives in Hungary as all communication was forbidden.

Lily Drágffy, Rachel, and Nicholas Drágffy at the 'Aeolus', late 1960s.

Lily died at Dreischor in the year 1980. Nicholas died in 1989 at Meppel, Netherlands. This was two years prior ro the fall of the Iron Curtain in 1991.

Gyula Drágffy (1906-1980), Rachel's father-in-law

Said Kati, her father Gyula:

'...graduated from a university of horticulture [the Royal School of Horticulture in Budapest] and at the outbreak of the war he was a horticulture technical school teacher.'

On 21 August 1940 Gyula married Edit Nagy (1920-1996), a teacher from Budapest. Edit was fond of literature, said her daughter Kati, and she possessed 'novels in Hungarian by English writers' such as Jane Austen.

In September 1944 Soviet forces entered Hungary and by 4 April 1945 the last German troops had been expelled from that country. Now came tragedy for the Drágffy family. 'Russian soldiers came', said Kati, 'took the watches and took civilian men to work, and raped women'. This was a reference to wristwatches and pocket watches. 'The Russian soldiers took the watches by force because they thought they were curiosities.'

'In our childhood house, there was a large shelter at the end of the garden, which was built of strong reinforced concrete. When the war broke out, Dad built it together with the residents. They took all civilians from the shelter because they needed labor. They didn't ask anything, they just took whoever they found.' And

Gyula Drágffy in 1932, in hunting attire! Photo: Gabriel Drágffy.

'Drágffy' coat of arms. Photo: Gabriel Drágffy.

Gyula and Edit Drágffy in 1941, with infant Gabor. Photo: Gabriel Drágffy.

one of the civilians abducted in this way was Gyula. 'As a civilian, he was illegally taken from the shelter to Siberia in 1945.' These abductions were all carried out by the Russian military. 'There were no Russian policemen.'

The Siberian labour camp in which Gyula was interred was part of the Gulag, a system of labour camps maintained in the Soviet Union from 1930 to 1955, in which many people died.[3] The Gulag agency was created by order of Lenin, and it reached its peak during Stalin's rule (1929 to 1953).

[Lenin (Vladimir Ilyich Ulyanov): head of the government of Soviet

Gyula in 1943. Photo: Katalin Kuchár.

Russia from 1917-1924 and of the Soviet Union from 1922-1924.

Joseph Vissarionovich Stalin: leader of the Soviet Union from 1924 until his death in 1953.]

Of the estimated 18 million people who passed through the Gulags, between 1.5 and 1.7 million died as a result of their incarceration.

'Apu [Daddy] never spoke about his ordeal,' said Kati. However, he did confide one piece of information to Rachel. Outside the wire fence surrounding his labour camp grew stinging nettles which he knew, as a botanist, were a source of vitamin C. Accordingly, when the guards were not looking, he reached throught wire and grasped some of the leaves, which he chewed. This action may have saved his life, malnutrition being endemic amongst the prisoners.

Gábor, Rachel, and Edit, Budapest, Hungary, winter 1964.

Gábor Drágffy, Rachel, and Gyula, Budapest, Hungary, 1964.

The dreadful conditions in the Gulags were graphically described by Russian writer and dissident Aleksandr Solzhenitsyn in *The Gulag Archipelago*, published in three volumes in 1973.

Gyula spent two-and-a-half years in the labour camp, said Kati, and he did not return home until 1948:

'He came home with a weight of 58 kg, we children did not recognize him. He was a very hardworking man with skillful hands, he made crucifixes and cutlery in his POW camp.'

Gyula died in 1980 at Siófok, Hungary, on the southern shores of Lake Balaton. Edit died in 1996.

Katalin ('Kati') Kuchár (née Drágffy, born 1943), Rachel's sister-in-law; and Ede Károly Kuchár (born 1930), Rachel's brother-in-law.

Kati met Charles (Ede Károly Kuchár), her husband-to-be at technical college where they were both studying electrical engineering and from which they both graduated with a diploma. In 1961, Kati and Charles were married. The following year, said Kati, 'we celebrated our one-year wedding anniversary in a motel in Balatonföldvár,' on the southern shores of Lake Balaton, and this was 'when my brother Gábor met Rae [Rachel].' In fact, Rachel and her parents had extended their visit to Hungary and were currently camping at Lake Ballaton. They had decided to visit the motel for a wash and brush up and a meal, as a special treat.

Kati and Charles found employment with Magyar ÁllamVasutak (Hungarian State Railways), Charles as a designer. As for Kati, 'I never worked as a designer,' she said, 'as our sons were born in the meantime, so I worked in the so-called non-production technical department.'

Rachel and her sister-in-law Kati developed a deep and lasting bond with one another. 'We all loved Rae very much,' she said:

'She was a very nice person who accepted the bad conditions in Hungary out of love and never complained about how much better she [had] lived in England. In Hungary, we called Rae "Kis Drágám" - "Little Darling".'

Rachel, Charles, Kati, and the author, Poole, Dorset, UK, Easter 2005.

'From what I was told by my in-laws, including Kati,' said Rachel, 'during the Second World War, people in Hungary were starving. Even Gábor's mother Edit, who was comparatively well off, used to walk miles into the countryside with a wooden trolley, to meet up with the peasants and trade her gold and jewellery for food.'

Said Kati, the Hungarian Revolution commenced on 23 October 1956:

'I was in piano lessons when we got the news that the university students had started the Revolution. I was only thirteen years old then.' In the course of the suppression of the Revolution by the Soviets, an estimated 2500 Hungarians died and more than 200,000 fled the country.

'When the Soviet troops invaded Hungary, following the uprising [Revolution] of October-November 1956, families were told that they were only permitted to have two rooms of their homes for their own use. The Drágffy family was therefore required to take in lodgers, with whom they had to share their bathroom and toilet. Even the basement, which had been a wood store and workshops was converted into accommodation for two families. The Drágffys were more fortunate than most, however. Valuable paintings hung on the walls, and it was only necessary for them to sell a single one of them in order to meet their outstanding tax liability.'

Aftermath

Following the end of the Cold War and the lifting of the Iron Curtain in 1991, Kati and Charles made several visits to the UK, Rachel and Gabor having divorced two years earlier in 1989. Here they were reunited with Rachel, and also with Rachel's mother Joan. 'When we were in London', said Kati, where Rachel showed her the sights, 'I heard the sound of Big Ben'.

'Big Ben' is the nickname for the Great Bell of the Great Clock of Westminster, at the north end of the Palace of Westminster in London, England. During the Second World War, the sound of the clock was an inspiration to the people of occupied Europe, Hungarians included, who heard it when, on their illicit radio sets, they tuned in to the BBC Home Service to hear the latest news on the radio.

At Easter 2005 Kati and Charles paid a visit to Rachel and me at our home in Poole, UK where I had the pleasure of meeting them for the first time.

After a few short months in Hungary, Rachel had learned to read, write, and speak the language fluently, even though this is acknowledged to be one of the most difficult languages to learn. And being welcomed into the bosom of her new Hungarian faily was an experience that she would treasure all her days. Years later, Kati would write:

'I remember very well when we were guests at your place and as long as I live, this memory will remain, and I am very grateful for the love we received from you.'

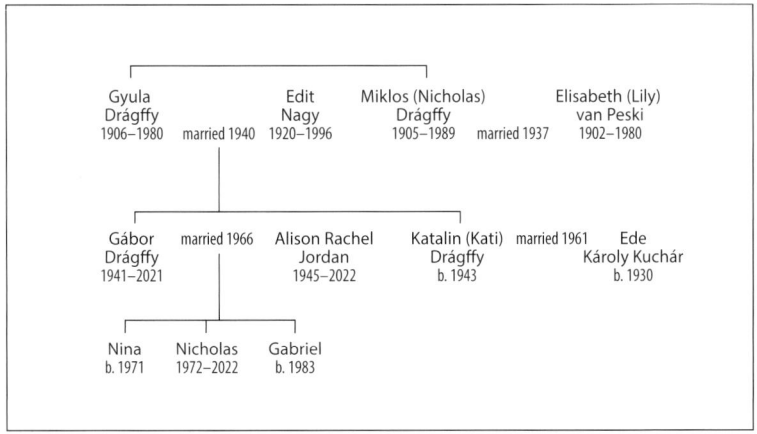

Drágffy family tree.

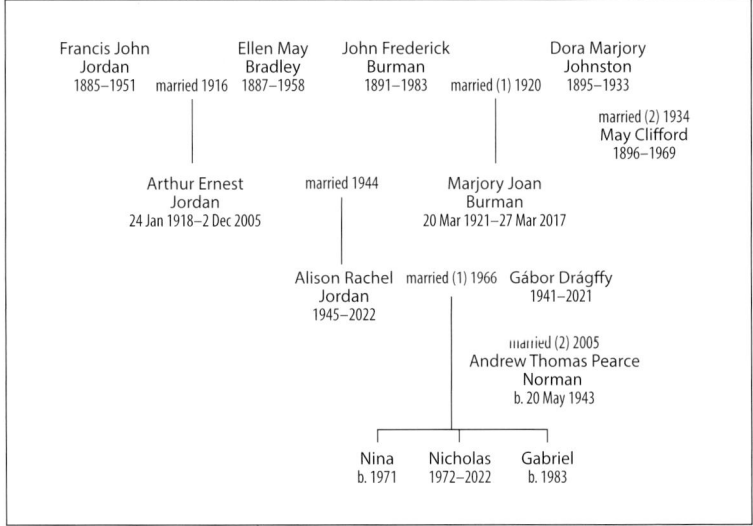

Jordan Family Tree.

[1] From the 'History of the Drágffy Family' by Gábor Drágffy.

[2] *Zierikzeesche Nieuwsbode*, 10 September 1982, pp.5-6.

[3] Stevenson, A., and Waite, M., *Concise Oxford English Dictionary.*

23

Escape!

In summer 1969, Rachel and Gabor left Hungary. Did Rachel leave Hungary because she found the conditions there intolerable? 'No, on the contrary. Conditions were fine for me. I had good friends and a lovely family of in-laws.' Did her husband, Gabor wish to leave? 'No. After all, he could have left in 1956.' That was during the Hungarian uprising, when some quarter of a million Hungarians had fled the country. 'We left because Gabor had been offered a job in Maidenhead, Berkshire, UK.'

'We left in secret, without even telling Gabor's parents. We took the minimum of possessions, contained in a couple of holdalls. We drove in the Renault Dauphine to the border, where the border guards made a few phone calls, and then they let us through. It was all a bit fishy really. It had probably been prearranged.'

'We arrived in the UK and rented the cheapest bedsit we could find in Reading, Berkshire, from where Gabor travelled the 15 miles to Maidenhead to work each day. He didn't need a work permit as he was married to me, but he had to wait seven years to become naturalised – that is, granted citizenship and be eligible for a British passport.'

'In summer 1970, Gabor was offered a job with an electronics firm in Falkirk, Scotland. Here all staff including managers were offered a new council house. Our daughter Nina was born here on 17 January 1971, followed by our son Nicholas ('Nicky') on 27 October 1972. Six months later, when we had saved up enough money for a deposit, we bought a detached house of our own in the nearby village of Wallacestone.'

'In summer 1977 Gabor was offered a job with an electronics firm in Swindon and we moved to Goatacre in Wiltshire. Here we remained, apart from a two-year sojourn in Munich eighteen months later.'

'On 12 May 1983, our third child, Michael, was born. In December 1984, I commenced a nurse retraining course at Swindon's Princess Margaret Hospital. We employed a nanny to look after Michael when I was away.'

'In 1985, when Michael was aged two, Gabor took him, Nina, and Nicholas to a dog breeder and they came back with a Hungarian Puli. We called him "Chocki".'

In November 1987, Rachel qualified as a staff nurse, and later as a sister specialising in ENT. She had finally achieved what she had set out do all those years ago as a student nurse at St Mary's Hospital, Paddington.

24

Life Under the Soviets
Arthur Hears the Truth

In 1969, the year when Rachel and Gabor left Hungary for good, Arthur had set up home with Elisabeth in the village of Gretton in Northamptonshire. They were married in June 1970.

Said Elisabeth, 'In the forty years I spent with Arthur he very rarely mentioned his life spent in Dorset with the Agricultural Workers Union. It seems he really wanted to wipe that out. He would share stories about his childhood, his time on the railway and during the war working with horses, but nothing until his move to Collets' in 1964. We spent a number of camping weekends in Dorset, but he would never take me to Tolpuddle, either for the annual "Rally Weekend" where the Tolpuddle Martyrs were commemorated or at any other time. Although he kept up his membership of the Communist Party and his readership of the *Daily Worker/Morning Star*, he did not attend meetings or take an active part.'

Arthur had extolled the virtues of Communism, so it was a curious twist of fate that his daughter should have married a Hungarian and gone to live with him in his home country, behind the Iron Curtain. The question is, did Rachel's experience of life in a satellite state of the Soviet Union match up to Arthur's rose-coloured vision, which was based on the limited experience of life under the Soviets, granted to him by his hosts when he visited Eastern Europe? The answer was an emphatic 'No'! Everything was dictated by the State.

'For example,' said Rachel, 'for the first three years of a baby's life the mother lived at home to look after the child, but on reduced pay. After that, her job was kept for her, but her wages ceased. There were sophisticated creches and nursery schools on practically every street corner, and it was the norm for every woman to go out to work.'

Rachel was aware that the local Communist Parties in the countries of Soviet-controlled eastern Europe which Arthur and the family had visited, has 'cherry picked' what the family was shown. For example, workers cheering and clapping to show how well they were looked after by the state. Thereafter, Arthur believed 'that everything was wonderful there. But I told him, "Daddy, it's not like that. The Hungarian people hate Hungary being a Russian satellite country where their leaders take all their instructions from Moscow".'

'A bus driver,' she said, 'got almost double the pay of a doctor, who has had six years training, and therefore the doctor was obliged to take tips and the Hippocratic Oath went out of the window! For the forthcoming birth of a baby, it was necessary to tip the obstetrician the equivalent of one month's wages. That was the going rate. The nurses too were paid very little and to survive, and they were also obliged to get their money from tips. If a patient in hospital said that he or she required an extra pillow in order to be comfortable, but did not have the money to tip, then no pillow would be forthcoming. It used to bring me to tears.'

'For hospital patients, the food they were offered was minimal, and they were dependent on their family to bring them adequate sustenance.'

'When you asked the doctor for a repeat prescription at the chemist, it was expected that you first put money in an envelope and slid it across the desk. If you went to a shop and asked for a pair of shoes, say size 38, the reply was invariably, "Sorry, we don't have that size". Whereupon, the customer offered the shop assistant some money and she would say, "I'll just go and check", and sure enough, the shoes were immediately forthcoming!'

'At home in the evenings, supper was fresh bread with salami, cheeses, and ham. However, if you asked the shopkeeper for "10 dkg" (10 decagrams, or 100 grams) or 3½ ounces, say, of cheese, he would first put an enormous piece of greaseproof paper on the scales and include the weight of the paper in the price!'

One wonders how Arthur, a keen tennis player, reacted when Rachel informed him that no tennis courts were permitted in Hungary, except on Margaret Island, Budapest, where there was a luxury hotel much frequented by foreigners. 'Tennis was considered to be a Western elitist sport,' said Rachel.

Finally, 'on special days, there were parades, and everyone had to go to the main square (Heroes' Square) in Budapest and wave flags. I never went!'

An account on the fledgling trade unions of the countries of Eastern Europe, and of what befell them after the invasion of these countries by the Red Army in 1944-1945, was provided by US economist and writer, Andrew Halasz in an article entitled 'Labor's Status in Iron Curtain Countries' and published in 1950:

'The Communists, in order to establish their control of labor, instituted trade union councils as the highest central organization of unions to represent labor with the government. Communists were placed at the head of these councils and in leading positions in the individual unions. The tactics by which the Communists established their grip on the trade unions was the same in each case. First, Communists were placed in top union positions in proportion to the party's representation in the coalition governments. Then these new leaders, using the political influence of the Communist Party and of the Soviet Union, expelled the old anti-Communist leaders from the unions and took over their control. In the union elections the Communist leaders presented the workers with lists of candidates for office prepared by the Communists, and by the use of pressure, threats, and force if necessary, compelled the members to vote for this list.'

In this way, the autonomy and independence of the fledgling trade unions in those countries was completely destroyed.

25

Joan in Retirement
Rachel Returns to Dorset

Joan worked for the MRC until her 60th birthday, 20 March 1981, when she retired. As a council tenant, she was now eligible to apply for a Greater London Council (GLL) flat in Dorset. In the following year of 1982, the NUAW was assimilated into the Transport and General Workers' Union as its Agricultural Section.

Joan chose to live in Swanage in a newly-built flat close to the seafront, into which she moved in 1983. Here she was reunited with former Dorset friends, including Helen Dunman and her children whose home, 'Cliff Cottage' overlooking Swanage Bay, was only a few minutes' walk away.

In her retirement, Joan led an active life. She became one of the 'Friends of [Swanage's] Durlston Country Park' where, on the 'Dolphin Watch' she recorded many sightings of dolphins. She also joined the Dorset Ramblers and the Swanage Railway volunteers, when she helped to clear brambles from the track in the very early days of the Swanage Railway Trust's formation, the aim being to re-create the age of steam!

Joan knitted many a woollen patchwork blanket which she donated to Oxfam. She also gave generously to charities, in particular Greenpeace and Friends of Durlston, and this, despite having limited resources of her own.

In 1988, Rachel attended that year's Tolpuddle Rally with a group of UNISON (trade union representing members from the public sector) members from Swindon's Princess Margaret Hospital where she worked

Joan retires from the MRC in 1981: with grandchildren Nina and Nicholas.

as a nurse. They travelled there by coach.

Rachel discovered that many changes had taken place. 'All the little village NUAW branches had been disbanded,' she said, 'there being no longer any agricultural workers left in the villages. And there were no union banners to be seen because there were no union branches left.' Furthermore, 'There was only one band, whereas we used to have three.'

In 1989 Rachel and Gabor were divorced. Rachel now set up home in Chiseldon, 3 miles from Swindon and within sight of The Ridgeway, an ancient trackway which traverses the chalk ridge of the Berkshire Downs. 'This was lovely country for dog walking,' she said, which Chocki appreciated, 'and the old railway lines had been made into a cycle track.'

Rachel (aged twenty-three) on Swanage beach in 1968, while she and Joan were staying with Helen Dunman at Cliff Cottage on the seafront.

Meanwhile, Rachel successfully completed the following courses: 'Update in Caring for People with Diabetes Mellitus' (25 November 1992); 'HIV/AIDS Awareness' (Lifestyle: Swindon Health Promotion Unit, 9 September 1993); 'Loss, Grief, and Bereavement' (4 November 1993); 'Learning and Helping Skills' (4 November 1993). These courses were run by the Bath and Swindon College of Health Studies.

Sadly, after all her efforts to retrain, and despite having been appointed nursing sister with responsibility for four hospital wards at the Princess Margaret Hospital, Swindon, Rachel was obliged to retire in 1994 at the age of forty-nine with health problems. Nursing had been her life's ambition, and this was heartbreaking for her.

In November 1994, Rachel and her youngest son Michael relocated to Herston, Swanage, to be nearer to her mother Joan, who had retired to Swanage fourteen years previously. Prior to the move, Michael, now aged eleven, stayed with his grandmother for six weeks in order that he could start at Swanage Middle School for the Autumn Term. 'Joan loved having him,' said Rachel 'and would take him in her car to Studland beach, or to Durlston Country Park where they spent a lot of time together.' As for Rachel's other two children, Nina had married Kevin and was living in Melksham, Wiltshire, and Nicholas was studying for his Master's Degree in Public International Law at King's College, London.

'Mummy was an independent person,' said Rachel, 'and we did not live in one another's pockets. We never discussed politics.' Why? 'Because I knew it would always end up in an argument!' said Rachel. 'However, she was very grateful that I was around in her later years.' This, surely, was an understatement!

What of Chocki? 'I used to take him for walks across the fields to Herston Halt,' said Rachel. This was a stop on the Swanage Railway, where the steam trains could be seen chugging up and down. 'That's as far as he would go.' Was he too old or unwell? 'I think he was just lazy!,' said Rachel. 'But Chocki responded to Mummy because she had a firm voice, and she gave him lots of treats.'

Joan with her Land Army Veterans' Badge.

Did Chocki enjoy swimming in the sea? 'Oh no! All Puli dogs hate the water. With their thick coats they become waterlogged and just sink in it. Even if there was only a little trickle of water, he avoided it. He liked the snow though.'

On 24 June 1996, Rachel was awarded her City and Guilds certificate in 'Learning Support' for children with 'Special Needs'. This course of study had involved her in travelling 30 miles to Weymouth for one evening per week. In this way, she was able to assist underperforming (or for that matter overperforming) children at Bovington Junior School.

In 2012, Rachel applied for the Women's Land Army Veterans' Badge for her mother Joan, who was delighted to receive it!

Joan and Rachel at Kingston Lacy amongst the snowdrops!

26

Rachel and I Meet
Marriage

I first met Rachel in summer 2002 at the Manor House Hotel, Studland. This was roughly halfway between our two homes: hers at Herston, Swanage and mine at Poole.

Rachel and I had coffee together and she offered to be 'mother'. But as she poured the hot milk into my cup, a small drop spilled onto the table. The waiter had to be summoned. He arrived with a bemused look on his face, enquired what the matter was, went to fetch a cloth, and removed the offending drop of milk with a somewhat sarcastic flourish! I deduced from this that Rachel was a stickler for hygiene. She subsequently informed me, when we had got to know one other better and she visited my bungalow, that she had never seen so much dust and so many cobwebs in all her life!

After coffee I asked her if she would care to take a stroll with me along the beach. She agreed, and we walked down the path to where exactly fifty-eight years previously, on 6 June 1944, Allied troops had prepared for the D-Day invasion of northern France, for this was the 6th of June 2002.

The author and Rachel on our wedding day, 12 May 2005.

It was a golden day which I would remember for the rest of my life, with the sun shining on Poole Bay and the Isle of Wight in the distance. We came to a wooden ramp used for launching boats, which had to be negotiated in order for us to continue with our walk. It stood about a foot above the beach and as I mounted it, Rachel very kindly took my hand to steady me. Up until that point, neither of us had revealed to the other

Rachel, recently married to Andrew at their home in Poole with Ann, her friend from childhood.

that we both had certain disabilities, mine the result of a 'slipped disc' which left me with residual sciatica in the right leg and hers, the result of fibromyalgia (inflammation of the muscles) which flared up from time to time, causing her intense pain. This gesture by Rachel left a lasting impression on me which I never forgot, and even though we had known each other for only an hour, it showed me that here was a caring person.

Another episode which remained indelibly imprinted on my mind occurred some days later. We had agreed to meet again and were crossing the road in Swanage when she linked arms in mine in a loving and caring way.

When Rachel told me that she had first arrived in Dorset in 1948 at the age of three, I could not resist teasing her gently by saying, 'So, you're not proper Dorset, then?'

It was my great privilege to be introduced to Joan, in whom I discovered that selfsame unselfish, caring, loving, and generous qualities that her daughter, Rachel possessed. We had many happy outings together and enjoyed many lovely Sunday lunches with her in Swanage – she prided herself on her 'roasties' – roast potatoes, browned to perfection! A game of Scrabble on a winter's day was a must! 'Trivial Pursuit' was played by all the family at Christmas and when the question was, 'Who succeeded Leonid Brezhnev as leader of the Soviet Union and Secretary General of its Communist Party?' everyone looked blank, except Joan, who gave the correct answer immediately: 'Yuri Andropov'!

In 2004, having learnt from Rachel that she and I were engaged to be married, Arthur, who was now aged eighty-six, wrote to her as follows in his usual humorous way: 'I didn't realise that people got "engaged" nowadays (except on the telephone).'

A month later, on 12 May 2005, Rachel and I were married. For her wedding dress, jacket, and hat, Rachel chose the colour pink, what else? She made the complete outfit herself! As for her bouquet, interspersed with white roses were what she described as 'dainty' pink wax flowers

Flying at Compton Abbas Airfield (left to right) Pilot, Michael, Nicholas, Joan, Rachel.

Rachel and Ann at the Wimbledon Tennis Championships, 2014.

(Latin name *chamelaucium uncinatum*). Finally, as if she had personally preordained it, the pink blossom of a cherry tree, in nearby Poole Park which was a backdrop to the wedding photographs, was in its full glory. As for myself, I wore a pink rose which she had given me, on my lapel. 'Rachel loves everything pink,' I said to myself, 'and cherishes it even more, because anything of that colour was denied to her as a child.'

One of the great joys of my life was to go with Rachel to Bryanston, where she had spent almost all of her childhood. Here, we met an elderly gentleman who was walking along The Drive and engaged him in conversation. 'You can tell he's a local,' said Rachel afterwards, 'by the way he pronounces "Bry-an-ston" – with an emphasis on the "an".'

A holiday at Lake Garda, 2006, Rachel conducting the orchestra!

27

A Visit to Tolpuddle
Pre-War Commemorations of the Martyrs

Rachel had told me, that her father had been the driving force behind the restarting of the Tolpuddle Rallies by the NUAW after the war. Before the war, it had been Arthur's predecessor, Fred James who had provided the inspiration for the inauguration of the first of the pre-war annual 'Tolpuddle Commemorations' in the year 1922. This event was subsequenty referred to as 'The Tolpuddle Demonstration', and finally 'The Tolpuddle Martyrs' Festival and Rally'. I decided to pay the village a visit. 'When you get back, I'll show you some photos,' Rachel promised.

I commenced my tour at the Memorial Cottages, located at the western end of the village on the Dorchester Road (which in the village undergoes a change of name to Main Road).

In 1932 the Trade Union Congress – TUC – a federation of the trade unions of England and Wales, instructed its General Council to organize a national Centenary Commemoration in recognition of the arrest and trial of the Tolpuddle Martyrs a century previously in 1834. (In previous years, the Dorset Organizer for the NUAW had supervised commemorations of the Martyrs locally.) To this end, a halfpenny levy was made on every member of a TUC affiliated union to provide the requisite funds. And

Memorial Cottages, Tolpuddle.

it was Walter Citrine, General Secretary of the TUC 'who shaped the commemoration from those vague beginnings in a Congress resolution.'

The outcome was, that in 1934, the centenary year of the Martyrs' arrest and trial, a row of six cottages were built on the western side of the village in their memory. The architect was Edward Unwin, with his father Sir Raymond Unwin as architectural consultant. Funded by the TUC, the cottages were to house agricultural workers in their retirement, and the local committee of the NUAW was given the task of finding and selecting the residents, who would live there free of charge.

Above each front door appeared the name of one of the Martyrs. 'A small room at the centre was designed as a common room, where residents could meet, read, show films, and use the one telephone.' At the rear were gardens, where the residents could grow vegetables and flowers, 'and orchards were planted at either end'.

A dedication ceremony to mark the opening of the Memorial Cottages was held on Friday 31 August 1934 in the presence of some 5000 visitors. There were speeches by the Chairman of the TUC Andrew Conley and by the Vice-Chairman A.G. Walkden. In his address to the crowd, Conley declared that the cottages would 'symbolise our homage to the Martyrs and form a pledge that we who consecrate and hallow this spot will maintain the principles they cherished and serve our course as they served it.' President of the NUAW, Edwin Gooch declared soberly that 'the days of martyrdom in the countryside were not yet over.' In other words, agricultural labourers were still suffering.

Members of the crowd were invited to inspect the cottages, with their 'modern amenities, which included running water, a heating system, and electric light. The stairs had a gentle gradient, and the bedrooms and living rooms were designed to be south-facing, in order that the occupants could enjoy the view and the sunshine.' The play, *Six Men of Dorset* was performed, and a medal struck. This was a play written by Poole railwayman and member of the rail union, Harry Brooks and adapted by actor and dramatist, Miles Malleson. It was published in 1934.

The common room has since become a museum in which are displayed historical photographs, documents, and other relevant artifacts.

In front of the cottages is a sculpture of a seated George Loveless with a backdrop of six stone pillars, one symbolising each Martyr. The sculpture, by Thompson Dagnall, was commissioned by the Tolpuddle Martyrs' Memorial Trust in 1984, the 150th anniversary of the Martyrs' arrest.

A short distance away, on the opposite side of the road to the Memorial Cottages, lies the Anglican parish church of St John the Evangelist.

George Loveless was born on 2 February 1797. His parents, Thomas Loveless and Dinah (née Stickland) had nine surviving children of whom he was the sixth. In this church George's father, Thomas, his mother, Dinah, he himself, and all his siblings were christened. And George was married here in 1824 to Elizabeth Snook by the vicar of Tolpuddle, the Reverend Thomas Warren. George subsequently became a Methodist and a Methodist lay preacher.

George Loveless by Thomas Dagnall, with the author. Photo: Barry King.

In the churchyard lies buried James Hammett; the only Martyr to live out his later years in his native land. On his return from Australia he worked in the building trade.

In 1875 the Agricultural Workers Union (predecessor to the NUAW) presented Hammett, who was now in his sixty-third year, with a purse containing gold sovereigns, a gold watch, and a testimonial which recorded 'the esteem and regard in which you

Michael, Rachel's son, at the grave of Tolpuddle Martyr James Hammett, 1988.

are held by us as one of the early Martyrs in the cause Unionism'.

On the same day that the Memorial Cottages were declared open, a ceremony was held to unveil a new headstone for Hammett's grave. Designed by sculptor, Eric Gill the headstone was partly paid for by the Building Workers' Union. Social reformer and leader of the Labour Party, George Lansbury gave the address, and prayers were said by the Methodist minister and by the Anglican vicar of Tolpuddle, Dr Thomas Warren.

(The Methodist minister has not been identified. Evidently, Methodists did not appoint a minister to each parish as the Church of England did. Instead, each of their ministers was attached to a circuit that covered several churches. Methodist preachers also conducted services.)

In old age, Hammett's eyesight began to fail and rather than be a burden to his family, he voluntarily entered the workhouse – a public institution in which the destitute of a parish received board and lodging in return for their labour.

The inscription on his tombstone reads:

JAMES HAMMETT
TOLPUDDLE MARTYR
PIONEER OF TRADES
UNIONISM, CHAMPION
OF FREEDOM
BORN 11 DECEMBER 1811
DIED 21 NOVEMBER 1891

Martyrs' Tree and Memorial Shelter, Tolpuddle. Photo: Trades Union Congress 1981.

On the village green stands the famous 'Martyrs' Tree', a sycamore which is more than 300 years old. It was under this very tree that the local agricultural labourers, including the six who would become known as the Tolpuddle Martyrs, met in 1834. At the base of the trunk is a plaque bearing the words:

'The Tree Council, in celebration of the Golden Jubilee of Queen Elizabeth II [6 February 2002], has designated the Martyrs' Tree one of fifty great British trees in recognition of its place in the national heritage. June 2002.'

Another sycamore, a sapling, was planted on The Green by Neil Kinnock, Leader of the Labour Party, in 1984, the 150th anniversary of the arrest of the Martyrs.

Also in 1934, a Memorial Shelter roofed with thatch was erected on the village green and, together with the Martyrs' Tree, was gifted to the National Trust, a registered charity, by businessman Sir Ernest Debenham. The shelter bears, on one side, the words: 'In Memory of the Dorset Labourers who made a Courageous Stand for

Tolpuddle, the Vicarage, 1901. Photo: Robert Heathcote.

Liberty in 1834'; and on the other side, the dates '1834' and '1934'.

Further along the road on the north side and set back is the Vicarage. According to George Loveless in his polemic *The Victims of Whiggery: A Statement of the Persecutions experienced by the Dorchester Labourers* (published in 1837), Tolpuddle's vicar, the Reverend Warren, promised to support the labourers in their claim for a living wage, only to betray them by subsequently denying it. A letter written by Warren in April 1834 is on display in the Tolpuddle Martyrs Museum. In it he said, 'these unions must be put a stop to, or the country will be together by the ears'. He also stated that villagers (angry at his treachery), had broken the windows of the vicarage.

Tolpuddle, the original Methodist Chapel, inaugurated 1818. Photo: Trades Union Congress and Tolpuddle Martyrs' Trust.

Taking time by the forelock I walked up the drive of the Vicarage, where a little girl was playing in the front garden. 'Is Mummy in?' I enquired. 'No.' 'Is Daddy at home?' 'Yes.' She fetched her father, who introduced himself as Robert Heathcote. I explained that I had been searching, without success, for an old photograph of the Vicarage. 'When I bought the property,' he said, 'I inherited some photographs. This is the oldest one. It hangs in the hall.' And there it was, on his smartphone, the building covered in Virginia creeper, with three ladies in the foreground and another standing in the doorway. 'You may use it, if you wish,' said Robert. 'I would date it to about 1880.' I was overjoyed!

Central to the lives of four of the Martyrs, namely the Lovelesses and the Standfields (James Brine became a convert to Methodism only later in life), and to many other villagers, was the Methodist Chapel, a Methodist being a member of a Christian Protestant denomination originating in the eighteenth century evangelistic movement of Charles and John Wesley and John Whitfield. In their time the four Methodist Martyrs would have taken pride in the building. Now it was, sadly, derelict and neglected.

In 1810, eight years prior to the building of the chapel, a 'Dissenter's Licence' (a licence which legitimised premises for use as a meeting house for dissenters – those who refused to accept the doctrines of the established Church) was first granted, 'for the dwelling place of Thomas Loveless'. Thomas was the father of George and James so it is likely that the brothers, and their other siblings of whom there were seven, were first guided towards Methodism by their father. The house of Thomas Standfield was also a venue for Methodist meetings.

Under the terms of a lease drawn up in September 1818, Martyr Thomas Standfield's father, Robert agreed to let a plot of land adjacent to his house to his son on a copyhold basis (i.e. for the period of one or more 'lives'

Martyrs' Gate (unveiled 1912), outside the 'new' Methodist Chapel, Tolpuddle. Photo by Dave Penman, Trades Union Congress and Tolpuddle Martyrs' Trust.

– lifetimes). This was so that Tolpuddle's first Methodist Chapel could be built on the site. The chapel was originally a single-storey building with a thatched roof. Its walls were built of cob, set on a brick plinth and decorated with flint course. It measures some 20 feet by 30 feet. The chapel appears as 'Plot 94: Methodist Chapel' on the 1843 Tithe Map for Tolpuddle, the landowners and occupiers being 'The Wesleyan Society'.

George Loveless was involved in the project from the very beginning, being one of the chapel's twelve trustees. Thomas Standfield was another of the trustees.

Lord Citrine, 1st Baron Citrine. Photo: Bassano Ltd, Wikimedia Commons.

Over the years, the following people also paid their respects to the Martyrs. In 1922 the Working Women's Club held a fête, and the club and the NUAW held a joint festival at Tolpuddle. In 1925 a party of workers from ASLEF, the train drivers and firemen's trade union, stopped in Tolpuddle to pay silent tribute at the Martyrs' Gate. In 1933, Labour Prime Minister Ramsay MacDonald visited Tolpuddle. In July 1934, David Lloyd George, leader of the Liberal Party, visited Tolpuddle and laid a wreath at the Martyrs' Gate.

Also in 1934, *The Book of the Martyrs of Tolpuddle* was published by the TUC, with contributors by TUC General Secretary, Walter Citrine; Labour MP, Sir Stafford Cripps; political theorist and economist, Harold Laski; Labour leader, Arthur Henderson; political theorist, G. D. H. Cole; English socialist economists and husband and wife, Sidney and Beatrice Webb; and Irish playwright and political activist, George Bernard Shaw.

When I returned from Tolpuddle, Rachel was as good as her word and out came her photograph album. 'Here are Mummy, Les Shears, and me taking a break during the 1960 Tolpuddle Rally. I was aged fifteen, and this was the first time I was allowed to have my hair permed! And here is Mummy at the 1988 Tolpuddle Rally, holding hands with Michael, aged five. And here is Michael again, during the same Rally, at the grave of Tolpuddle Martyr, James Hammett.'

I now gave Rachel a surprise when I showed her a photograph of myself and the Rt Hon. Tony Benn, taken at the 2006 Tolpuddle Rally.

Taking a break at the Tolpuddle Rally, 1960. Left to right: Joan, Les Shears, Rachel (aged fifteen). 'This was the first time I was allowed to have my hair permed!'

The author and the Rt Hon. Tony Benn at Tolpuddle Rally.

28
Arthur's Role in the Rebirth of the Tolpuddle Rallies

Much as the hierarchy of the NUAW would have liked to expunge Arthur from the history books, his achievements as its Organizer for Dorset and his role in reviving the Tolpuddle Rallies are undisputed.

Said Rachel, 'Daddy provided the inspiration, energy, enthusiasm, and organizational skills to get the Tolpuddle Rallies restarted after they had lapsed during the Second World War.' So why was Arthur so passionate about preserving the memory of the Martyrs? For the same reasons as he wished to help the agricultural workers of his time, of course.

An article in *Land and Labour* stated that Arthur was not only 'the Tolpuddle Martyrs Rally organizer', he was also 'a regular speaker at the event, galvanising it into a memorable and permanent feature of the Labour Movement's calendar.' And Tony Gould, former District Organiser in Kent for the NUAW, confirmed that it was Arthur 'and members of the Dorset Area Committee who established the Rally on a permanent basis after the Second World War.'

Less than 5% of the minutes of the Dorset County NUAW Committee, and of the Dorset NUAW Branch Committees survive. But even from these records it is clear that Arthur was heavily involved with the post-war Tolpuddle Rallies – which in the early days were called the 'Tolpuddle Demonstrations'.

For example, on 6 October 1960, under the heading 'Tolpuddle Demonstration', the minutes of the Shaftesbury and Gillingham Committee state that 'Bro [brother]. Jordan called for full support from the branches to make the occasion a mighty Trade Union Demonstration in support of the Union's demands.'

On 17 December 1960, to the Dorset County NUAW Committee, 'Bro. Jordan read a letter from the [NUAW] General Secretary setting out a programme for the 1961 [Tolpuddle] demo and notifying that the TUC speaker would be Bro. E. Hill of the Boilermakers Society.' This was Edward J. Hill, General Secretary of the Boilermakers Union (1948-1965) and later President of the TUC.

On 3 June 1961 it was agreed in respect of 'The Tolpuddle Martyrs Demonstration' that 'the Chairman should be Bro. L. [Les] Shears and that the Organizer [Arthur Jordan] should be among the speakers as in previous years. It was confirmed that the Committee would organize the sale of refreshments, subject to securing the cooperation of the ladies who assisted last year.'

On 22 July 1961, under the heading 'Tolpuddle Martyrs Demonstration', 'The success of this year's demo was noted. A number of suggestions for improving the arrangements in future were made and endorsed by the committee as follows: 1) that the Old Crown Court at Dorchester [where the Martyrs were tried and convicted] should be opened for stated times and these times be included in the publicity material; 2) that a better quality handbill be produced in future; 3) that a number of official stewards should be appointed, and supplied with an armband or a badge; 4) that the procession be better arranged with [marker] pegs in the bank to indicate where banners should be hoisted.'

On 7 October 1961, to the Dorset County NUAW Committee, 'Bro. Jordan' presented a report on the catering arrangements for that year's Tolpuddle 'Demonstration', which 'had showed a small profit. It was decided to record appreciation to the ladies who served refreshments and to invite them with their husbands to the County Dinner.'

29

Other Events Relating to the Martyrs

The *Country Standard* described itself as 'The progressive journal for rural communities since 1935'. It's motto was, 'Sharpen the Sickle! The Fields are White; 'Tis the Time of the Harvest at Last'. The issue for 24 June 2010 contained an article entitled 'Tolpuddle – London 1948':

'Three hundred Dorset men and women,' one of whom was Arthur, 'marched through the streets of London on Sunday 20th March 1948 to honour the Tolpuddle Martyrs, who had 114 years previously been sentenced to transportation for founding a trade union. [In fact, the Martyrs were convicted for swearing an illegal oath.] Mrs E. Richardson of Dorchester, a niece of George Loveless, one of the men transported was also present.'

'Mr Stark of Affpuddle carried the Tolpuddle banner, and Mr J. Lovell the Dorchester banner. Other Dorset banners included Broadwey, Halstock, Puddle Valley, Cerne Abbas, Puddletown, Bloxworth, Whitechurch, Blandford, Witchampton, Tarrant Rushton, and Kingston. The original Tolpuddle banner was, on inspection, found to be too tattered to be brought.' Posters on the march bore such slogans as 'Homes not Hovels'; 'We demand £6 for Farm Workers'; 'We grow your food. Help us get justice'.

'They held a brief meeting in Trafalgar Square where Arthur Jordan stated that he hoped that the Londoners realised the farm workers were as class-conscious as they were.' Said Arthur:

'The Tolpuddle martyrs were sentenced for taking an unlawful oath … today there are martyrs in Whitehall [location of the various governmental departments] who are to be persecuted for holding political views with which the dominant classes do not agree.'

'The marchers, all members of the Dorset NUAW, were also treated to a special performance of the play, *Six Men of Dorset* performed by the Unity Theatre.

On 10 March 2007, the *Country Standard* carried an article entitled 'Dorset NUAW Banner 1955':

'The new and striking banner of the Dorset NUAW was unveiled during luncheon by Harold Collison, General Secretary of the NUAW, at the Dorset conference of the NUAW held in Poole on Saturday 29th October 1955.'

'The banner cost over £100, the sum being donated by members in Dorset.'

'The Dorset NUAW banner was designed by Mr E. Brooks and was considered to be revolutionary in design. The design had two figures depicting a farm labourer of the period of the Tolpuddle Martyrs in shackles, and a hand sickle and a modern farm worker, spanner in hand, stepping forward with his modern tractor in the background.'

30

The Post-War Tolpuddle Rallies
Rachel Remembers

One day, I heard Rachel discussing the Tolpuddle Martyrs with her mother Joan. 'Did you know that it was Daddy who got the Tolpuddle Rallies restarted, after they had lapsed during the war?' she said. So, Arthur's spirit lived on, in the county of Dorset that he loved so much. This knowledge left me with a burning desire to discover more, not only about the Tolpuddle Martyrs' Rallies and their origin, but also about the so-called Tolpuddle Martyrs in whose honour they were held. And this I did, with Rachel's invaluable help.

The post-war Tolpuddle Rallies traditionally took place, annually, in the third week in July. In 1946 the first post-war Rally since before the war, organized by Arthur, was held. The Whitechurch Silver Band led the march and Sidney Dye, Labour MP for Norfolk addressed the gathering.

In 1947 the Tolpuddle Rally was attended by some 6000 people, including German prisoners of war who had not yet been repatriated and were working on the land. Speakers included Edwin Gooch, President of the NUAW and now Labour MP for North Norfolk; Alfred C. Dann, General Secretary of the NUAW; George Chester from General Council of the TUC; and Hugh Dalton, Labour Chancellor of the Exchequer who promised land workers a fair deal.

By 1948 the Tolpuddle Rally had become a festival, which according to the *Country Standard*, 'began on the Thursday with an Old Time Dance in Dorchester's Corn Exchange. Friday saw a Variety Concert and on Saturday a 200-strong march took place in Dorchester led by the London Workers' Pipe Band. Events included gymnastics, a horticultural show, and athletic competitions. On Sunday Edwin Gooch and Alfred Dann spoke of the massive growth in the NUAW. 70,000 workers had joined that year, 500 in Dorset in the previous six months.'

'I attended every Tolpuddle Rally from the age of four,' said Rachel, beginning in 1949. On 19 May 1949 it was recorded in the minutes of the NUAW Dorset County Committee, under the heading 'Tolpuddle Sunday', that: 'This will be a great day for the Dorset workers. Book the date. Sunday

July 17. Special – *Six Men of Dorset*, the play about the Tolpuddle Martyrs. Two performances were given in a tent which seated 2000. Seats bookable. Speakers Tom Braddock MP; E. G. Gooch MP; A. C. Dann, General Secretary [NUAW]; F. [Fred] Brown, EC [NUAW Executive Committee] member.'

'It was a big event in the calendar,' said Rachel, 'and it was always a wonderful day. Every village had its own banner, made of beautiful silk, 3 to 4-foot long and narrow, carried on a single pole which fitted into a leather pouch attached to the bearer's belt, and with the emblem of the National Union of Agricultural Workers – the NUAW – and the name of the branch. There was only one two-pole banner, born by two men at the head of the procession, and that was the Dorset NUAW banner. And it was always Daddy and the invited guests who led the procession.'

'There were two brass bands, one at the front and one at the rear. The procession made its way from the Memorial Cottages to the churchyard of the parish church of St John the Evangelist where Martyr Hammett is buried. Everyone remained on the road, apart from the leaders of the procession and the invited guest, who laid a wreath of laurel leaves on Hammett's grave. (Daddy ordered the wreath each year from the florist in Blandford.) Helen Dunman was there. Her professional name was Helen Muspratt. She was a friend of Mummy's, and she took lots of photographs.'

'When we returned to the Memorial Cottages the banners were put away, and the bands played. Whereupon two large marquees were erected on the lawn: the beer tent and the tea tent. And everyone was served with a cup and saucer, not mugs. I was there helping. I was in charge of a big freezer box containing ice creams. I would lift the lid, take out whatever variety they wanted, and take the money. You could also buy sandwiches.'

'Long tables were erected in front of the Memorial Cottages and the guest speakers all spoke and Daddy made his speech. Then everybody dispersed back to their coaches.'

'Mummy always made and served the teas, along with Jess Waterman's wife Norma, and Glad [Gladys] Shears. Glad's husband, Les would arrive at events on a motorbike, with Glad in the sidecar! Les was a Communist sympathiser, but he never joined the Communist Party. Glad and Mummy were friends for many years. And there was always a jumble sale with proceeds going to the union.'

'And Jess?'

'Jess was NUAW Branch Secretary for Spettisbury, Dorset. Jess and Ernie Amey, Branch Secretary for Farnham, Dorset, were very close with Daddy. They did a lot together, to do with the union.'

'Were either Jess or Ernie members of the Communist Party,' I asked Rachel.

'Nobody was,' she replied. In other words, Arthur, as a Communist, was ploughing a lone furrow!

'Labour politician and trade unionist Joan Maynard was also a great friend of Mummy's, and she too attended the Rallies, where she was the main speaker.'

In that year of 1949 a number of Communists with banners joined Tolpuddle Rally procession, with the result that NUAW President Edwin Gooch and NUAW General Secretary Alfred Dann refused to take part in it. Gooch also refused to speak at the following years' Rally.

'Do you think Arthur encouraged the Communists to join the Rally?' I asked Rachel. 'Definitely not,' she replied at once. 'Had he done so he would have been sacked on the spot!' Nevertheless, the furore that this caused is born out by a 'Report', sent by Arthur as Organizer, 'to all Dorset Branches, District Committee Secretaries, and County Committee members' dated 12 September 1949 and kindly made available to me by Tom de Wit, Manager of the Tolpuddle Martyrs Museum. Under the heading 'Meeting of the Dorset County NUAW Committee held Saturday 10 September 10th 1949 at Tolpuddle,' Arthur described how:

'A total of branches had sent in resolutions regarding the incident caused by the President [Edwin Gooch] on July 17th. Wareham branch strongly criticised Bro. Gooch for deserting the Union; [Winterborne] Stickland branch asked for an enquiry; whilst the Dorchester, Piddletrenthide, Winterborne Abbas, and Owermoigne branches made accusations against the Dorset leadership. There was a discussion on [i.e. about] Tolpuddle Sunday in which Bro. Lovell of Dorchester branch admitted that he had tried to persuade branches to withdraw their banners but only three did so. Bro. Jordan produced a letter which had been written by Mrs Riggs, County Committee member to branches in the Bridport district urging them to demand the dismissal of the Organizer [i.e. Arthur himself!].'

The outcome was the passing of the following resolution:

'That this Dorset County Committee, having considered letters from certain branches, states clearly that they have every confidence in their Organizer, Bro. Jordan, and that neither the County Committee nor the Organizer can be held responsible for the presence of Communists on Tolpuddle Sunday.' The vote was 'For 6: Against 1, with 1 abstention'.

Nonetheless, Arthur had addressed his aforementioned report to 'Dear Comrade', which was a traditional greeting of one communist to another, instead of to 'Dear Brother', which was the traditional trade unionist greeting. Dorset farm worker John Fry also objected to being addressed as 'comrade' by Arthur. 'I thought, brother, fair enough, but he would call me comrade,' he said. Nevertheless, said Fry, 'Arthur' really believed in what he was doing – that he could help his fellow man.'

Little Rachel, aged four, was probably completely unaware of all these shenanigans!

In 1951 when Labour MP, Tom Driberg and National Executive member of the NUAW, Fred Brown addressed the Rally, it was reported that 'only 200 people' were present.

Tolpuddle Rally, July 1988. Joan at front beneath 'Farnham Branch, Dorset County' banner, holding hands with Rachel's son, Michael.

Prior to the 1952 Rally it was reported that some Labour leaders had objected to Arthur's presence. At this, in the *Western Morning News* edition of 3 May 1952, Brown expressed his indignation:

'From information in my possession, it appears that some of the leaders of the Labour Party have been attempting to interfere in a matter which I consider concerned only the union — a domestic matter, which should not concern the Labour Party. Further, it appears that these leaders were prepared to boycott the union's demonstration [Rally], unless the union executive accepted their demand and barred the Dorset union official [i.e. Arthur] from being on the platform. It seems that leaders of the NUAW are prepared to allow this interference in what, I insist, is a union matter alone.'

Three days later, in the *Dorset Echo* edition of 6 May 1952, it was reported that Fred Brown had resigned from both the union and from the Labour Party:

…'in protest against an alleged threat of Labour Party Headquarters to boycott the demonstration if Communist officials of the union appeared on the platform.'

Brown had served the Labour Party and the NUAW for almost fifty years. Arthur responded to this by saying:

'My membership of the Communist Party has been widely known among the members of my union for several years, but the rank and file members have more than once indicated that they will judge me by my success as a union organizer and extend to me the same political tolerance which the union extends to its members.'

'This unprecedented discrimination against a Trades Union's officer by the Labour Party leaders should be a warning signal to all who have the interests of the working class at heart, for Red-hunting to-day will be Bevan-hunting to-morrow, as we have seen in America.' This was a reference to Labour Party politician, Aneurin Bevan. In the early 1950s, Bevan was leader of the left-wing of the Labour Party, whose members became known as 'Bevanites'.

'I can say that the NUAW in Dorset will support the Labour Party but will not tolerate the "big stick" interference of organisations; to which the union is affiliated. Fortunately, the majority of the rank and file Labour Party members are more tolerant than their leaders.' Sadly, for Arthur, however, the clouds were gathering.

Nevertheless, the 1952 Tolpuddle Rally, presided over by Jess Waterman, the NUAW County Chairman, went ahead as planned, with Arthur as usual playing a pivotal role and making a major contribution. Reports of the Rally appeared in various editions of the *Dorset County Chronicle*:

'Motor coaches from a dozen different points in the South of England converged on Tolpuddle on Sunday afternoon for the annual Tolpuddle Martyrs demonstration. One coachload came from as far west as Penzance and others came from Sussex, Hampshire, Wiltshire, Devon and Somerset.'

'On the lawn of the Memorial Cottages one could see nicely dressed, healthy-looking mothers with their young children. Family parties with jacketless men in open-necked shirts brought their own picnic baskets and sat in the shade, while others patronised a marquee for tea, cakes and sandwiches, manned mainly by wives and friends of the Dorset branch of the Agricultural Workers' Union.' One of the wives, undoubtedly, was Arthur's wife, Joan, with Rachel, now aged seven, in attendance.

'During the leisurely mustering of the assembly the band played pleasant Sunday afternoon music on the lawn, but it gave way to political speakers after the march had been completed.'

Another account of the 1952 Rally was published in the *Dorset Echo*:

'In temperatures in the 80s, the banners were carried aloft, and with pride. The band from Wyke Regis led a procession, nearly 200 strong from the Trade Union Congress Memorial Cottages down the dusty road to the village, where the President of the National Union of Agricultural Workers, Mr E. G. Gooch, MP for North Norfolk, walking under the red, blue, and gold banner of the union, paid his tribute to the memory of the pioneers.'

'These pioneers of the trade union improvement started something which, to show a proper appreciation, had to be carried on. In the forty-six years of existence the NUAW had achievements to its credit, such as George

Loveless, the leader of the six, and his friends could never have dreamed of. But the work had to be continued.'

It was now Arthur's turn to make his contribution to the proceedings, and it was a major one. 'The previous day in Dorchester, he said, he and his colleagues put up a good, sound and-logical case to justify a claim for a minimum wage of £6 a week for agricultural workers. They put up a really, powerful case but it only took the farmers five minutes to say no. They [the farmers] had no argument; they had no case. All they could say was no, they could not afford it.'

The Central Agricultural Wages Board's offer 'of a mere five shillings a week increase', said Arthur, was 'totally inadequate in view of the ever rising cost of living. Neither would the proposed new wage attract men to the land to help the vital expansion of food production. He criticised the Tory Government's handling of the economic situation and said the last Budget had made wage claims inevitable.'

'He had no doubt that further restrictions were to come and with them, further appeals for wage restraint. The farm workers should not be fobbed off with an increase which bore no relationship with the cost of living, he added.'

Nevertheless, 'It was inspiring, he went on, to read about Helsinki and the Olympic Games. There, all political differences were sunk, and the hand of friendship extended. There was no Iron Curtain and there were no political barriers — just young people taking part in sport. If that was possible in Helsinki, he said, it was possible all over the world.' Once again, this was Arthur the idealist speaking!

'Mr A. C. Dann, General Secretary of the NUAW, said they needed to recapture the spirit of the Tolpuddle Martyrs. He was followed by other speakers, before the demonstration finally broke up.'

Two press reports, however, indicate that the Labour Party hierarchy was displeased with the Rally and had indicated its displeasure in no uncertain way. The *Bristol Evening News* edition of 21 July 1952 carried the headline, 'Labour Leaders Boycott Tolpuddle'. And in the *Poole Herald* edition of 23 July 1952, it was stated that:

'Labour Party representatives were absent from the Tolpuddle Martyrs demonstration in Dorset on Sunday (20 July 1952). They were said to have boycotted because Communists were on the platform.'

In 1953, Harold Collison, the newly appointed General Secretary of the NUAW, addressed the Rally, and again in 1954 and 1956. Collison would one day be Arthur's nemesis.

31

Where in Tolpuddle did Each of the Martyrs Live, and By Whom Were They Employed?

Having got to know the village of Tolpuddle reasonably well, I now set about trying to discover the whereabouts of the homes of the six Martyrs and of the farm where they worked. In this, two sources of information proved invaluable. Firstly, the Tithe Apportionment Map for Tolpuddle of 1843, where all the properties and fields are numbered with a key indicating the name of the landowner; that of the occupier; and a brief description. In those days, one tenth (or tithe) of a person's annual produce or earnings were taken as tax to support the church and clergy. Secondly, the 1841 Census for Tolpuddle (the first modern United Kingdom census),

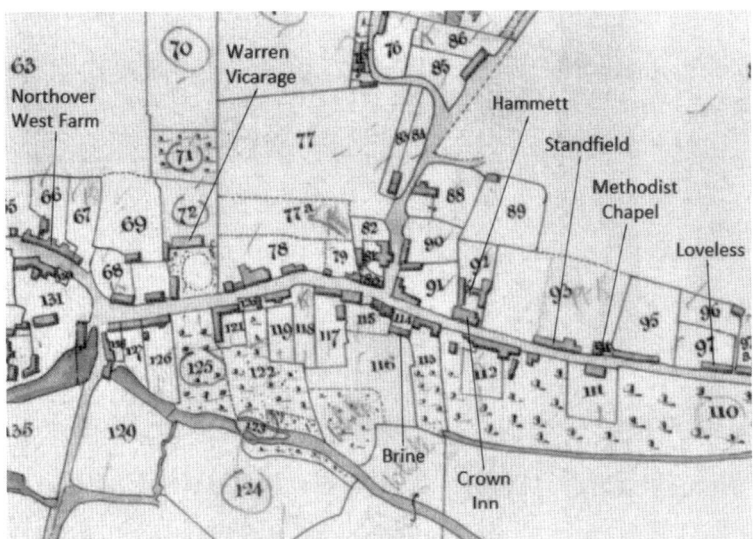

The abodes of the the Tolpuddle Martyrs, Farmer Susanna Northover and the Reverend Thomas Warren, prior to the arrest of the Martyrs in 1834. After the Tithe Apportionment Map 1843, Courtesy Dorset History Centre.

taken seven years after the arrest of the Martyrs but, nonetheless, a supply of useful information.

Thomas and John Standfield

The home of Thomas and John Standfield, a semi-detached two-storey cottage on the north side of Main Road is easily identified by the memorial plaque on the wall. It reads as follows:

'Dedicated by the Trade Union Congress to the Memory of the Six Agricultural Labourers of this village whose trade union meetings in this cottage led to their being sentenced to seven year transportation in 1834.'

This is recorded as 'Plot 93: Two Tenements and Land' (of which the Standfield family occupied one tenement) on the Tithe Map.

James Hammett

A copy of a letter, kindly provided by Warwick University Records Centre, refers to the fact that James Hammett was arrested (prior to his trial in 1834) 'at cottages in the rear of the Crown Inn'. (The inn was destroyed by fire, and a new inn built on the site. In 1979 it was named 'The Martyrs' Inn'.) The cottage has since been demolished.

This is recorded as 'Plot 92: Tenements & Garden' (of which the Hammett family occupied one tenement, another being the Crown Inn itself) on the Tithe Map.

James Brine

William Puckett of Dorchester, a relation of the Hammetts, writing on 15 January 1934 to Walter Citrine of the TUC, stated that 'the cottage in which James Brine lived ... is directly opposite the present public house.' To my disappointment, however, I found no sign of the cottage, only two semi-detached bungalows which had been subsequently built on the site. Taking the initiative, I asked the owner of one of the bungalows, Ron Ricketts, if he remembered the cottage. Yes, he said, it had fallen derelict and was demolished

James Brine's former cottage (front), opposite the Martyrs' Inn. Photo: Ron Ricketts.

James Brine's former cottage (rear). Photo: Ron Ricketts.

in the 1960s. Did he have a photograph of the cottage? He would look and see, and if he found one, he would give it to Tony Gould, a near neighbour, who would post it to me in Poole. It was therefore a great joy when, a week or two later not one, but two photos arrived for me in the post of the old, thatched cottage, a front view and a rear view!

This is recorded as 'Plot 113: Cottage, Garden & Orchard on the Tithe Map.

George and James Loveless

For me, the 'Jewel in the Crown' would be to discover where the Loveless family and, in particular, where the Martyrs, George and his son, James had lived.

On 4 March 1816, Thomas Loveless signed a copyhold lease (based on tenure for a life or number of lives, as opposed to an ordinary lease which could be renewed at intervals with the consent of both parties) for a cottage and garden. The property occupied an area of 30 perches (⅕ of an acre or approximately 1000 square yards) for which the annual rental was 15 shillings. The lease was to

The only known image of George Loveless.

run for the lives of Thomas himself, then aged fifty-five, and of his sons, George aged eighteen, Samuel thirteen, and James eight. (The four older siblings had already left home.) When Thomas Loveless signed the above lease for his property, James Northover, farmer at East Farm, Tolpuddle for whom he worked, was present as a witness. East Farm and West Farm were the two main farms in the village.

On 31 December 1933, Frank Hammett, who was related to the Loveless family, wrote to Walter M. Citrine General Secretary of the Trade Union Congress (Lord Citrine from 1947) saying, in respect of where the Loveless family might have lived, 'I think I have heard my mother say it was the cottage occupied in my boyhood days by Thomas Cross, situated on the left-hand side after passing the village well [presumably when walking eastwards through the village]'.

Tolpuddle's village well is situated almost opposite the original Wesleyan Chapel and 10 yards, or so, back from Main Road. The well is now sealed off, but the arm holding the pump handle remains. The cottage referred to was, therefore, on the north side of the road.

Tolpuddle's Tithe Map of 1843 indicates that the Cross family did, indeed, occupy a cottage in the village. It stood on Plot No. 97; the landowner being William Cross and the occupiers were Richard Cross, labourer, and others.

From the Tithe Map, it is evident (by extrapolation from the plot opposite, whose area is specified on the map in acres, roods, and perches) that the size of Plot No. 97 was almost exactly 30 perches or 1/5 of an acre. This figure corresponds precisely with that given in the aforesaid lease for the plot, signed by Thomas Loveless in 1816. Finally, none of the other plots in any way approximate to these dimensions.

From the Tithe Map it is also possible to calculate the relative distances between Whitehill Lane (leading north off Main Road), East Farm, and the 'Cross' family cottage on Plot No. 97. The distance from Whitehill Lane to the western end of East Farm is 88 paces. From the Tithe Map, the expected distance from East Farm to the 'Cross' family cottage is 200 paces.

When these distances are paced out, this brings a great surprise. There is, indeed, a property at the location in question – so-called 'Pixies Cottage' – an ancient, listed (i.e. protected) building. It appears, therefore, beyond reasonable doubt that this was where the Loveless family, including brother Martyrs George and James lived. Finally, yes, the cottage is situated beyond – i.e. to the east of the village well.

This is recorded as 'Plot 97: Three Tenements and Garden' on the Tithe Map.

The next question is, for whom did the Martyrs work, and on what farm?

Susanna Northover

Martyr Thomas Standfield's father, Robert leased a cottage from James Northover of East Farm. When Martyr Thomas Loveless, father of George, signed a lease for his cottage, James Northover was a witness.

James Northover was born in 1776. On 10 October 1800 he married Susanna Pont of Fordington, Dorchester who bore him five surviving children. On 2 February 1819, Susanna took out a lease on West Farm, Tolpuddle. James Northover died in 1822 (and subsequently the tenant of East Farm was a William Brine). It is likely, therefore, that George and James Loveless, Thomas and John Standfield, and also James Brine and James Hammett were all employed by Susanna Northover of West Farm. The farm is located on the south side of Main Road, adjacent to the Parish Church.

At the time of the Martyrs' arrest in 1834, Susanna Northover was aged forty-eight and living with her four children: Elizabeth twenty-one;

William (who subsequently became the village miller) eighteen; James seventeen; Rebecca thirteen.

West Farm is recorded as 'Plot 131: Farm House, Barns, Dairy House, Buildings & Yard', on the Tithe Map. It is also recorded that Susanna Northover's landlord was the Reverend Edward St John Senior; that her total holding was 546 acres (or just under 1 square mile), mainly located to the west of the village. This included barn and barton (farmyard); eweleaze (sheep pasture); cowleaze; lambing plot; marling pits (marl – soil consisting of clay and lime used as fertiliser); pasture; willow bed (branches of willow are harvested annually in autumn when the tree is dormant, to make baskets); a horse close (enclosed paddock); and a hop yard (where the hop plant grows up along strings supported by big, strong wooden poles – a hop plant lives for about thirty years, the hops are picked around September and the smell is intoxicating). Also, a spear bed (for raising asparagus or broccoli); warren (enclosed piece of land reserved for breeding game); and a water mill. Susanna's holdings also included five cottages and four tenements.

The vast majority of working men in the village were, like the Martyrs, agricultural labourers. There were also dairymen, brick makers and bricklayers, a blacksmith, a journeyman (one who is paid by the day and not bound by indentures – i.e. a contract); a carrier (for conveying goods by horse and cart), and a shoemaker.

The Reverend Thomas Warren

Tolpuddle Vicarage is located on the north side of Main Road, to the east of the parish church. This is recorded as 'Plot 72: Vicarage House, Lawn & Garden' on the Tithe Map; the landowners being 'The Dean & Chapter of Oxford'.

In 1834 the Vicarage was occupied by the aforementioned Reverend Thomas Warren, vicar, aged sixty-four and his two female servants: Mary Tizzard aged twenty-nine, and Emily Stermey aged eighteen.

The Crown Inn

According to the 1843 Tithe Map, Tolpuddle's publican was John Bullen, married to Anna. He was both the Landowner and the occupier of Plot 92, which comprised 'Tenements & Garden'. One of these tenements was occupied by James Hammett; another was the Crown Inn itself (as already mentioned).

32

A Visit to Dorchester
Scene of the 'Crime'

In the last week of August 1934, a four-day Commemoration of the Martyrs took place in Dorchester. This included a grand procession with football and tennis competitions, a brass band, tugs-of-war, international athletics, dancers from abroad in national costume, and writing competitions. Also flower shows and a motorised carnival procession, with decorated floats that were judged by the Countess of Warwick. The play, *Six Men of Dorset* was once more performed.

Rachel and I decided that it was time to visit Dorchester, the scene of the 'Crime', that crime being not principally the swearing by the Tolpuddle Martyrs of an illegal oath in 1834. The real crime was their unnecessarily harsh treatment of arrest, conviction, and transportation by the powers that be, using this as a pretext.

At the 'Top O' Town', in North Square, is the gaol where the Martyrs were imprisoned. Built in 1785, its original, intimidating, massive stone-built arch still remains. The prison overlooks the River Frome, and on the opposite bank is the ominously named 'Hangman's Cottage'.

Facing High West Street, on its north side, is the Old Shire Hall, a late eighteenth century courthouse built of ashlar stone, housing the former Crown Court, scene of the Tolpuddle Martyrs' trial in 1834. Two wall plaques bear testimony to the Martyrs. The first bears the inscription:

In this Building
On March 19th 1834
The Six Tolpuddle Martyrs were Sentenced
To Seven Years Transportation
For Their Part in the Founding
Of Rural Trade Unionism

Unveiled by Alderman E. G. Gooch C.B.E, J.P. M.P.
President of the National Union of Agricultural Workers
July 1947

'Daddy was present when the plaque was unveiled,' said Rachel.

The second, a hexagonal bronze plaque in relief by Ian Homer Walters, depicts the Martyrs in chains beneath the famous Tolpuddle sycamore tree and surrounded by agricultural produce. It was commissioned by Dorchester Town Council in 1984, the 150th anniversary of the Martyrs' trial.

In the basement of the Shire Hall are the cells, including the small, single room in which the Martyrs were imprisoned, described by George Loveless as 'a miserable dungeon'.

The courtroom in which the Martyrs were tried has changed little over the years and here it is before our very eyes. The judge sat beneath the Royal Arms of King George III (father of the reigning monarch, King William IV), from which the court derived its authority. Alongside the judge were benches reserved for court recorders and trainee judges. Below him, in the well of the court, sat the counsels for the defence and for the prosecution. In the enclosed gallery, to the left, were seated the 12 members of the jury.

The gallery above, to the judge's right, was reserved for friends of the judge, and also for members of the Grand Jury who wished to attend. A raised platform at the far end of the court, opposite the judge's seat, was set aside for members of the public, of whom there were many, there being great interest in the proceedings.

In the centre of the court was the raised dock, in one of the side panels of which was a small door. If a prisoner was declared to be innocent, the door would be unlocked to allow him or her to walk free. In the case of the six men, however, the door would remain firmly locked.

In 1955 the Shire Hall ceased to be a court and was henceforth used as offices for West Dorset District Council. However, in 1956 the TUC created a charitable trust which purchased the courtroom and cells from the council. The TUC now became custodians of the Old Court: one of the trustees being General Secretary of the NUAW, Harold Collison.

Bronze plaque in relief by Ian Homer Walters, Old Shire Hall, Dorchester, commissioned by Dorchester Town Council in 1984.

In 1968 the TUC decided to return their part of the building to its previous owner, provided that: 'The Council hereby covenant with the Trustees [to] keep [the courtroom] open for public inspection at all reasonable hours in the daytime on weekdays.'

33

The Return of the Martyrs

When the sentence was passed on the Tolpuddle Martyrs, this was greeted by a national outcry and trade unionists began to organize a campaign to have the six men released. The Tolpuddle Museum website contains an excellent account:

'A vast demonstration took place on 21st April 1834. Up to 100,000 people assembled in Copenhagen Fields near King's Cross [Central London]. At Whitehall a petition, borne on the shoulders of twelve unionists, was taken to the office of the Home Secretary, Lord Melbourne.' Melbourne, however, 'hid behind his curtains and refused to accept the massive petition.' More petitions came from all over the country, the total number of signatories being in excess of 800,000! Meanwhile, the trade unions supported the Martyrs' families by collecting donations and kept the campaign going until the Government relented.

'By June 1835, ten months after the Martyrs' arrival in the penal colonies, conditional pardons had been granted by Lord John Russell, the Home Secretary.' However, the Tolpuddle six refused to accept conditional pardons, 'and after further pressure, the Government agreed on 14th March 1836 that all the men should have a full and free pardon.'

George Loveless returned to England on 13 June 1837. James Loveless, Thomas and John Standfield, and James Brine returned nine months later on 17 March 1838. Meanwhile James Hammett was detained at Windsor, New South Wales on an assault charge. He did not arrive back in England until August 1839.

Hammett returned to his home village of Tolpuddle. The other five men and their families set up home at two farms in Essex, paid for by the 'Dorset Labourers' Farm Tribute', a fundraising campaign launched by the London Central Dorchester Committee – established to raise funds to buy or rent small farms for pardoned men.

The Reverend Henry Walter, Vicar of Hazelbury Bryan in North Dorset, criticised George Loveless for his views. Whereupon, in February 1838, Loveless, a highly intelligent, self-educated, and articulate person, addressed a pamphlet entitled 'The Church Shown Up' to Walter in the form of a letter. It began with a quotation from the poet John Milton:

'Give me the liberty to think, to speak, and to argue freely according to conscience, above all other liberties.'

It was Loveless's view, that the 'first great object[ive]' of the labouring classes must be to achieve their 'emancipation from mental and political slavery'. How were these aims to be achieved? By the 'increased spread of knowledge', which would soon 'scatter its healing, saving, and benign influence over and around the darkness and ignorance of the human mind ….' Finally, having learnt that union strength, and knowledge is power, the poor labourers would unite 'in all their moral dignity, shake off the trammels of despotism', and demand their just rights.

In spring of 1844 George and James Loveless and James Brine and their families emigrated to Canada. In 1846, Thomas Standfield and his family, including his son John, followed suit.

It was not until 1867, under the recommendations of the Royal Commission, that trade unions were finally decriminalised. In that year, the Trade Union Congress – TUC – was founded. In 1871, the Trade Union Movement was legalised, and in 1872, trade unions themselves were legalised.

As historian, Clare Griffiths so rightly points out, the Tolpuddle Martyrs are now regarded 'as the forebears of all trade unionists, whatever their occupation'.

34

Arthur in Retirement
Education; Books; Steam Trains

Arthur retired from Collets in 1978. Prior to this he had become involved in taking the occasional class with the WEA. This now developed into almost a full-time job, said his wife, Elisabeth. He became a tutor specialising in railway history, and from 1980 he lectured at Leicester University on subjects as diverse as road and canal history and mediaeval social history. He also secured an Open University degree to make up for his 'dreadful' childhood education.

Arthur's book, *The Stratford-upon-Avon and Midland Junction Railway: The Shakespeare Route* was published on 1 August 1982. In it, he described how one day, when he was working on his model railway, which occupied the entire garage of his house, and listening to the radio, he heard someone criticising how history is taught in schools. Such history, said the critic, was:

'...mainly about kings and queens and prominent persons, but little or nothing is taught about the history of the people, ordinary people like ourselves, who contributed so much to history and human progress.'

'It occurred to me,' said Arthur, 'that the same can be said for railway history.' In his book, he would therefore 'set out to capture the atmosphere of everyday life on an average railway station.' And he would do this by 'by drawing upon my own knowledge and experience gained on a cross country railway in the years before the Second World War.'

In fact for Arthur, this was an experience which had begun long ago, said Rachel, ever since he was a little boy, in fact, 'when the engine drivers at Stratford-on-Avon would sometimes take him with them for a ride in their cabs, a fond memory which remained with him all his life.'

In his second book, *Away for the Day: The Railway Excursion in Britain, 1830 to the Present Day*, published on 30 August 1991, which he co-authored with Elisabeth, Arthur demonstrated his concern for the underprivileged and especially for children.

'Excursion trains (taking passengers on trips for leisure activities) of any kind were opposed by those seeking to preserve their exclusiveness, but the strongest, the most virulent opposition was directed against the Sunday excursion, and this mainly on religious grounds. Yet, for the majority of workers in factory, office, shop, or on farms, Sunday was the only toil-free day in their lives.'

Arthur explained how the granting of leisure to the working classes had been an agonisingly prolonged process, in its evolution:

'A weekly early-closing day for shopworkers was not introduced before 1911, whilst for factory work the so-called half-day on Saturday meant a finish at 2 p.m. under the Factory Act of 1850. The Bank Holiday Act was not passed until 1871, and paid annual holidays for most workers was not achieved until between the two World Wars. So, it was a case of the Sunday excursion or nothing.'

'In the lives of many Victorian, Edwardian, and prior to that even Georgian children their most memorable day was the annual trip to the seaside or the country. The Sunday School outing was, for most children their only outing of the year; eagerly awaited, long remembered.' The Sunday School was a class which preceded the regular Sunday church service at which children were given religious instruction.

'It was the railways which opened up new horizons for the organizers; whilst for the children a ride on a train was an occasion for great excitement, as was their first encounter with the sea and sand which the railways made possible for many landlocked city dwellers.' Doubtless, in the back of his mind, Arthur was thinking of his beloved daughter, Rachel and remembering their trips to the seaside together with her mother, Joan.

'Arthur was not a reader of fiction,' said Elisabeth, 'but he possessed a collection of books from the Left Book Club (founded in 1936 to oppose war, inequality, and fascism) and a complete set of Thomas Hardy's novels. He also collected books on railway history, including a complete set of bound copies of *Railway Magazine*. Later in life, however, he started reading Agatha Christie and Conan Doyle.'

'With regard to music, the radio in Arthur's study was permanently set to the BBC Third Programme. He also enjoyed Traditional Jazz and had a collection of weird and wonderful music from South America and Africa!'

35

8 April 2005
Arthur and Rachel are Reunited: I Meet Arthur for the First Time

Rachel and I duly drove up to Northamptonshire and stayed in a hotel in Stamford. The reunion went wonderfully well, and the look of joy on the faces of both Rachel and her father as they embraced was unforgettable.

A postcard sent to Rachel following the reunion depicted 'Touching Souls', a sculpture by Romanian sculptor Mico Kaufman symbolising universal peace and reconciliation.

Rachel had taken a photograph of Arthur's model railway and sent it to her father, together with my biography of T. E. Lawrence. In May 2005 he wrote:

'Dear Rachel, Thank you both for the album of photos which makes a visible record of our memorable reunion after thirty-seven years. I still cannot believe that you, the mature mother of adult children, are the same little girl that I once played with round our ex-army hut, on the beach, and later as a teenager on the tennis courts.'

Rachel with Arthur and his train layout, Gretton, Northamptonshire, 8 April 2005.

'The shots of the model railway make a record of it in a state of its construction. If it is ever finished, you must photo it again. I enclose my comments on L of A [*Lawrence of Arabia*] after reading Andrew's excellent book. We must keep in touch Rachel. Much love and regards to Andrew, Daddy.'

I wondered, subsequently, if in a quiet moment, Arthur had broached the thorny subject of politics to Rachel. The answer was no. 'I'm surprised Daddy never asked me,' she said. 'Maybe he felt it was too early. Maybe he would have done at a later date.' Alas, there was to be no 'later date'.

8 APRIL 2005: ARTHUR AND RACHEL ARE REUNITED: I MEET ARTHUR FOR THE FIRST TIME

Arthur died at his home in Gretton on Friday 2 December 2005 aged eighty-seven years. His funeral service was held at 10.30 a.m. on Tuesday 13 December at the Gretton Village Hall, followed by internment at Ketton Park Green Burials.

Rachel and I attended the funeral, as did his widow Elisabeth. The chosen hymn was 'Jerusalem', with lyrics by William Blake and set to music by William Parry, its final verse being:

I will not cease from mental fight,
Nor shall my sword sleep in my hand,
Till we have built Jerusalem
In England's green and pleasant land.

How appropriate, I thought, for a person who had done and tried to do so much for others during his lifetime. In the following speech, Rachel paid this tribute to her father:

'It seems rather strange that I have actually known my dear father for less time than probably most of you gathered here today. And yet I feel so very lucky, that for the first nineteen years of my life I have such lovely memories of a truly happy childhood, and of a father, who despite his loyal commitment to his demanding work as a trade union official, always made time for me and the significant events taking place in my life.'

'Although I was a lone child, I was never a lonely child. Looking back, as we all do, I cherish his love and his guidance of those formative years.'

'Sadly, for some forty years we "lost" each other – and I missed his fatherly love so very much. But, dearest Daddy, in April this year, with the support of your dear wife, Elisabeth and my dear husband, Andrew we were reunited – and for this I am eternally grateful.'

'I treasure your last words to me: "Please, don't be sad Rachel. Be happy for these wonderful past hours we've shared, and for the memories. I love you very much."'

For Rachel, the past was the past, bygones were bygones, and all that mattered was that she had been reunited with her father, and that they had been able to reaffirm their deep and abiding love for one another.

'What are your views on politics, bearing in mind what you have told me about your upbringing?' I ventured to ask Rachel. 'I don't really take an active interest,' she replied, 'because I can't be bothered with it all. I know what I think is right and wrong and who is doing the right thing or not. I have never joined a political party. I think politicians are all a load of rogues.' Then, with a smile, she said, 'But if everyone was like me, we'd never get anywhere, would we.'

Epilogue

Rachel gave a unique insight into post-war life in rural Dorset and introduced me to the glorious countryside where she spent almost all of her childhood. She also told me how she had been brought up by loving parents and the evidence was there for all to see.

In nineteenth-century Dorset, George Loveless (and the five other Tolpuddle Martyrs and many others) were motivated to take action out of sheer necessity, in that their families were literally on the brink of starvation. The Martyrs lived their lives against the backdrop of the French Revolution of 1789 to 1799, which took place less than half a century prior to their arrest on 24 February 1834. The authorities were, therefore, likely to come down hard on anyone suspected of being a revolutionary.

In the twentieth century, when agricultural labourers in the UK were still living in poverty, Arthur Jordan as a trade unionist did his utmost to improve their lot. But this was in the teeth of opposition. Arthur himself, operated in an environment in which the authorities were apprehensive about the growing influence and power of the trade unions. He was opposed by the farmers, naturally, but he was also up against 'monopoly capitalism', whereby big business held the reins, aided and abetted by the Government. In fact, he came to believe that no political party, not even the Labour Party to which he had once belonged, were capable of addressing the inequalities in society which he strived to redress. This is why he became a Communist.

But being a Communist made Arthur's task more difficult, especially at the time of the 'Cold War' (which commenced in 1947 and ended in 1991), a period of ideological and geopolitical tension between the US and the Soviet Union and their respective allies. He was, therefore, looked upon with a mixture of suspicion and opprobrium.

In common with George Loveless, Arthur believed that the current establishment was an abhorrent instrument of repression, and had the two men been contemporaries, they would undoubtedly have been soulmates – apart from the fact that the former was a devout Methodist and the latter was an atheist!

The Tolpuddle Martyrs suffered by being uprooted from their native land and transported to Australia, where they lived under the harshest of conditions. Arthur suffered from being hounded out of the job which he loved and which he had devoted his life to.

The Tolpuddle Martyrs have become immortal figures in the history of trade unionism, and Arthur's legacy is to have kept their memory alive, by providing the impetus, enthusiasm, and energy to re-establish the Tolpuddle Rallies after the Second World War. The Rallies are now an important part of the social calendar, dear to the hearts of trade unionists everywhere, but also dear to the hearts of all decent and fair-minded people of goodwill.

Arthur Jordan (who, together with his wife, Joan) was a member of the Communist Party, was a dreamer or, as his daughter, Rachel said, an idealist, and why not? He believed that life for the agricultural workers in England and in the UK would be better under a Soviet socialist system then under capitalism. But there were other reasons for Arthur's love for and admiration of Soviet Russia.

As a musician and a music lover, Arthur would have been enthralled by the music of Russian composers such as Rachmaninov, Mussorgsky, Prokofiev, and countless others. The music of Tchaikovsky, in particular, seems to speak to all of humanity from the very soul of Russia itself. Furthermore, in Tchaikovsky's ballets, which both Arthur, Joan, and Rachel had seen performed by the Bolshoi company of Moscow, these may be regarded as the most sublime of all the art forms that the theatre has to offer.

In a greeting card to Rachel, Arthur expressed his hope for 'PEACE in our world'. Surely, he longed for peace between the nations, and with Russia in particular, instead of the mistrustful and sometimes fraught and dangerous relationship which the west and the east have now.

As regards the reality of day to day life under the Soviet system, Rachel knew better than her father, having gone to live behind the Iron Curtain during the Soviet era. Here, nurses, doctors, and others depended on receiving bribes to make ends meet, the black market flourished, enterprise was discouraged, and the inefficient, creaking system was self-perpetuating. But Rachel and her father would certainly have agreed that the faults of both east and west lay with their systems of government/ideologies, and with the greed, corruption, and criminality of their leaders, and not with people such as those who Rachel came to know and love in Hungary.

What of Arthur's hope that his daughter, Rachel would grow up to 'help people and make a better world'. By becoming a nursing sister, and by numerous acts of kindness, both in this capacity and in all other aspects of her life, she most certainly fulfilled her father's wish! And I, for one, am eternally thankful for having met and married her, and for having my life immeasurably enriched by her.

Index

Aldermaston March 61
'And Quiet Flows the Don' 53
Amey, Ernie 71, 114
Andrews, George 38
Andropov, Yuri 100
Atlee, Clement 65
Arch, Joseph 14-15
Australia 18, 42, 83, 104, 132
Away for the Day: The Railway Excursion in Britain, 1830 to the Present Day 128

Bartlett, Miss 19
Benn, Tony 61, 108
Bere Regis 17
Bevan, Aneurin 117
Blandford Forum (Blandford), Dorset 7, 17, 20-21, 24, 27, 29, 34-36, 38, 41, 44, 48, 60, 71, 114
Blandford Forum Town Museum 23
Blandford Trades Council 37
Blunt, Anthony 26
Bolshoi Ballet 59, 133
Book of the Martyrs of Tolpuddle, The 107
Boult, Adrian 60
Bournemouth Symphony Orchestra 59
Braddock, Tom 114
Brezhnev, Leonid 100
Brighton 59
Brine, James 18, 106, 120, 122, 126-127
Bristol Evening News 118
Brooks, Harry 103
Brooks, Mrs 44-45
Brown, Frederick ('Fred') 114, 116
Bryanston, Dorset 7, 17, 19, 21-24, 34, 41, 43-44, 46-47, 75, 101
Bryanston Camp 24
Bryanston School, 22, 48
Budapest, Hungary 65, 78, 80-81, 83, 85, 94
Burgess, Guy 26
Burman, Dora Marjory (née Johnson) 10-11, 90
Burman, John Frederick 10-11, 90
Burman, Marjory Joan 10, 12, 90
Burnham, Thomas 10

Campaign for Nuclear Disarmament (CND) 26, 61
'Chocki' 91, 97-98
Chester, George 113
Church of St John the Evangelist, Tolpuddle 103, 114

Church of St Nicholas, Durweston 44
Citrine, Walter 103, 107-108, 120-121
Clifford, May 11
Cole, Frederick 74
Cole, G. D. H. 108
Collets bookshop 75, 93, 128
Collison, Harold 72-74, 112, 118, 125
'Common Market' (European Economic Community) 69, 71-72
Communist Party of Great Britain 28, 69
Conley, Andrew 103
Coombes, Maurice 19
Coombes, Peg 19
Coombes, Tony 48
Copenhagen Fields, King's Cross, London 126
Country Standard 25, 29, 72, 111, 113
Crown Hotel, Blandford 22, 54
Cripps, Stafford 108
Czechoslovakia 63, 65

Dagnall, Thompson 103-104
Daily Worker 93
Dalton, Hugh Dann, Alfred C. 113
'D-Day', 6 June 1944 24, 99
Dominey, Betty 19
Dominey, Ivor 19
Dorset County Chronicle 117
Dorset Echo 116-117
Dorset Standard 31
Drágffy, Gabor 65, 75-76, 78, 80-82, 84, 86-91, 93, 97
Dragffy, Gyula 80, 85-87, 90
Drágffy, Michael 91, 97, 101, 104, 108, 116
Dragffy Miklos (Nicholas or Uncle Miki) 83-85, 90
Drágffy, Nicholas 90-91, 97, 101
Drágffy, Nina 90-91, 97
Driberg, Tom 116
Dunford, Ann 19, 47
Dunford, Ellen 19, 77
Dunford, John ('Johnnie') 19, 77
Dunman, Helen (née Muspratt) 25-26, 77, 96, 114
Dunman, John ('Jack') 25-27, 30, 33
Dunman, Lisa (née Griffin) 25
Dunman, Percy 25
Durweston Primary School, Durweston, Dorset 43, 45
Dye, Sidney 113

INDEX

Eastern Counties Agricultural Labourers and Small Holders Union 15
East Germany 52, 63-65
Engels, Friedrich 29

Fleming, Alexander 67
Frampton, James 49
Fry, John 116

Gamba, Pierino 59
George III, King 125
Gill, Eric 104
Gooch, Edwin G. 39, 73, 103, 113-115, 117, 124
Gould, Tony 109, 121
Griffiths, Clare 127
Groves, Charles 59
Groves, Reginald 14
Gulag Archipelago, The 87

Halasz, Andrew 94
Hall & Woodhouse Brewery 41
Hammett, Harriet (née Gibbons) 18
Hammett, James 18, 104, 108, 114, 120, 122-123, 126
Harper's Bazaar 75-76
Harrison, F. 9
Henderson, Arthur 108
Higgs, Clyde 9, 12, 16
Hodsdon, Dennis 30
Huebner Clarence R. 24

James, Fred 36-37, 102
'Jipp' 46, 62, 76-78
Joplin, Scott 60
Jordan, Arthur Ernest 7-8, 30, 35, 37, 39-40, 70-74, 90, 110-111, 115, 132-133
Jordan, Ellen May (née Bradley) – 'Nanny Jordan' 8, 16
Jordan, Elisabeth (née Frood) 75-76
Jordan, Francis ('Frank') John 8-9, 16, 22, 90
Jordan, Marjory Joan (née Burman) 10-12, 90

Kaufman, Mico 130
King Edward VI Grammar School, Stratford-on-Avon 8
Kinnock, Neil 105

Land and Labour 39, 68, 70, 72, 109
Landworker 71
Lane, Albert 41, 48
Lane, Mavis 41, 48
Laski, Harold 108
Lawrence, T. E. 130

Livingstone, Ken 76
Lloyd George, David 34, 107
London Central Dorchester Committee 126
Loveless, Dinah (née Stickland) 104
Loveless, Elizabeth (née Snook) 18
Loveless, George 17-18, 103-104, 106-107, 118, 121-122, 126-127, 132
Loveless, James 18, 106, 121-122, 127
Loveless, Samuel 121
Loveless, Thomas 106, 121
Lunnon, James ('Jimmy') 33

MacDonald, Ramsay 107
Maclean, Donald 26
Malleson, Miles 103
Martyrs' Gate, Tolpuddle 107
Martyrs' Inn (formerly 'The Crown') 120, 123
Martyrs Memorial Cottages 102-104, 114, 117
Martyrs' Tree, Tolpuddle 105
Marx, Karl 25, 29
Maynard, Joan 73, 115
Medical Research Council 76
McGill, Miss 60
Melbourne, Lord 126
Memorial Shelter, Tolpuddle 105
Morning Star 93
Morse, Ken 20
Muspratt, Helen (see Dunman)

National Agricultural Labourers and Rural Workers Union (NALRWU) 15, 33-34, 37
National Agricultural Labourers Union 15
National Farmers Union 69
National Union of Agricultural and Allied Workers 15
National Union of Agricultural Workers (NUAW) 7, 9, 15, 17, 19, 25-26, 29-30, 33-40, 49-50, 52, 54, 69-74, 77, 79, 96-97, 102-104, 107, 109-118, 125
National Youth Orchestra 57, 60
Northover, James 121-122
Northover, Susanna 119, 122
Number 8, Forum View, Bryanston, Dorset 46, 54, 60, 74, 77
Number 8, The Cliff, Bryanston 19, 24, 43

O'Connor, Kristine Mason 30, 73
Peters, Leonard 24
Poole Herald 118
Portman Estate 19, 22, 34, 43
Princess Margaret Hospital, Swindon 91, 96-97

Ramsay, Lettice 26
Rhondda Valley, South Wales 26
Royal Albert Hall 60
Royal College of Music 60
Russell, Bertrand 61
Russell, John 126

Semmelweis, Ignaz 13
Shaw, George Bernard 108
Shears, Glad [Gladys] 77, 114
Shears, Les 77, 108, 110, 114
Sholokhov, Mikhail 53
Solzhenitsyn, Aleksandr 87
Stalin, Josef 29, 65, 87
Standfield, Dianne (née Loveless) 18
Standfield, John 18, 120, 122, 126-127
Standfield, Thomas 18, 107, 120, 122, 126-127
Stratford Memorial Theatre 16
Stratford-on-Avon and Midland Junction Railway 8, 128
St Mary's Hospital, Paddington 66-67, 75-76, 92
Sue Barton: Student Nurse 67
Swanage, Dorset 25, 27, 77, 96-97, 100

'The Cranes are Flying' 52
The Crown (see the Martyrs' Inn)
The Stratford-upon-Avon and Midland Junction Railway: The Shakespeare Route 128
Thomas, Edward 10
Tithe Map of Tolpuddle, 1843 107, 122-123
Tolpuddle Martyrs' Memorial Trust 103
Tory, John 23
Tory, Philip 23, 34, 41
Trade Union Congress (TUC) 39, 102-103, 107, 109, 113, 120-121, 125, 127
Transport and General Workers' Union 96

Truman, Harry S. 65

Unwin, Mr 45
Unwin, Edward 103
Unwin, Raymond 103
US 1st Infantry Division ('The Big Red 1') 23-24

Van Diemen's Land (now called Tasmania) 18
Victims of Whiggery, The: A Statement of the Persecutions experienced by the Dorchester Labourers 106

Walter, Henry 126
Warman, Bill 40
Warren, Thomas 104, 106, 123
Waterman, Jess 39, 74, 114-115, 117
Waterman, Norma 114
Webb, Sidney 108
Webb, Beatrice 108
Wellesbourne, Warwickshire 8-9, 14
Wesley, Charles 106
Wesley, John 106
Western Morning News 116
Weymouth, Dorset 30, 49, 52, 62, 98
Whitfield, John 106
William IV, King 125
Williams, Baron 18
Williams, Nancy 60
Wilson, Harold 20
Winterborne Kingston 19, 77
Winterborne Stickland 43
Winter Gardens Bournemouth 58-59
Women's Land Army 11, 20, 98

Zedong, Mao 46